BRAIN

D1435249

MIND-BENDING PUZZLES

TERRY STICKELS

P PUZZLE WRIGHT PRESS

New York

PUZZLE
WRIGHT
PRESS

New York

An Imprint of Sterling Publishing
387 Park Avenue South
New York, NY 10016

PUZZLEWRIGHT PRESS and the distinctive Puzzlewright Press logo
are registered trademarks of Sterling Publishing Co., Inc.

© 2013 by Terry Stickels

Parts of this book were previously published under the titles
Mind Workout Puzzles and *Mesmerizing Mind-Bending Puzzles*
© 2001 and 2002 by Terry Stickels

ISBN 978-1-4549-0963-7

Distributed in Canada by Sterling Publishing
c/o Canadian Manda Group, 165 Dufferin Street
Toronto, Ontario, Canada M6K 3H6
Distributed in the United Kingdom by GMC Distribution Services
Castle Place, 166 High Street, Lewes, East Sussex, England BN7 1XU
Distributed in Australia by Capricorn Link (Australia) Pty. Ltd.
P.O. Box 704, Windsor, NSW 2756, Australia

For information about custom editions, special sales, and premium and
corporate purchases, please contact Sterling Special Sales
at 800-805-5489 or specialsales@sterlingpublishing.com.

Manufactured in the United States of America

2   4   6   8   10   9   7   5   3

www.puzzlewright.com

CONTENTS

INTRODUCTION

The puzzles in this book have one sole purpose: for you to have fun. These brainteasers may be solved many different ways, so please don't think there's only one way to solve them. One way is given in the answer section, but your way may be just as valid.

You'll find word games, math brainteasers, spatial/visual puzzles, and other mind treats, giving you diversity while you stretch your mind and increase your mental flexibility. If you've had a little algebra, you'll find it useful in solving some of the puzzles, but don't worry if you haven't ... it's not mandatory. These puzzles are meant for both beginners and advanced puzzle solvers.

There's no time limit for any of these puzzles. Take as long as you like or skip to another puzzle and come back later to the one that has you stumped. You'll be amazed how quickly your mind starts piecing things together.

Good luck and happy puzzling!

1

For the uninitiated, the next three puzzles are called cryptarithms or, more precisely, alphametics. Puzzle creator J. A. H. Hunter coined the term *alphametic* to designate words that have meaning, rather than the random use of letters found in cryptarithms.

The object of this type of puzzle is to replace letters with digits. Each letter must represent the same digit, and no beginning letter of a word can be zero. If properly constructed, alphametics can be deduced logically.

In the first puzzle, my verbal arithmetic leaves something to be desired. Assign a number to each letter to correct my addition. Hint: Make a box or chart to consider the possibilities of different values.

$$
\begin{array}{r}
\text{ONE} \\
\text{ONE} \\
\text{ONE} \\
+\ \text{ONE} \\
\hline
\text{TEN}
\end{array}
$$

2

$$
\begin{array}{r}
\text{NOON} \\
\text{MOON} \\
+\ \text{SOON} \\
\hline
\text{JUNE}
\end{array}
$$

3

This third alphametic is more difficult than the first two, and there is more than one correct answer. Hint: create more than one chart of values.

```
    THIS
      IS
     NOT
+   WITH
─────────
   WHICH
```

4

If B + P + F = 24, what are the values of Q and T? Hint: Consider whole numbers only.

$$A + B = Z$$
$$Z + P = T$$
$$T + A = F$$
$$F + S = Q$$
$$Q - T = 7$$

5

Here is a cube presented from five different perspectives. One of the views is incorrect. Can you tell which one?

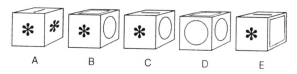

A   B   C   D   E

6

Here is one way to unfold the cube in puzzle 5.

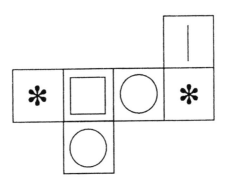

Here are two other ways to unfold a cube.
How many additional ways can a cube be unfolded?

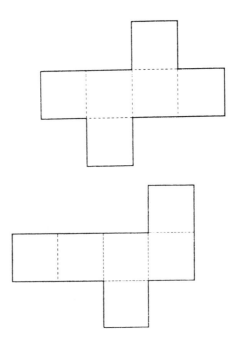

7

Your boss has asked you to purchase three different types of ballpoint pen. The first costs 50¢, the second $5.50, and the third $9.50. He has given you $100 and told you to purchase 100 pens in any combination as long as you spend exactly $100 for 100 pens. Just one solution is possible. Can you find it? Hint: Familiarity with solving simultaneous equations would be helpful here.

8

Three of these five figures fit together to create a triangle. Which ones are they?

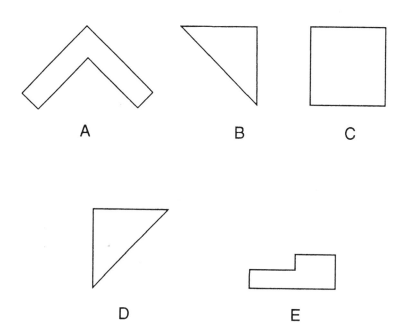

9

Here's a problem that will test your "layered thinking" ability. Give yourself about a minute to solve this puzzle.

Imagine that you have four kings and three queens from an ordinary deck of playing cards. (If you have access to a deck, the puzzle is more fun.)

The object of the game is to arrange the seven cards in an order that will result in an alternating pattern of K, Q, K, Q, K, Q, K. The seven cards must be held facedown. Move every other card, beginning with the first, to the bottom of the deck. Beginning with the second card, place every other card faceup on the table to reach the desired alternating pattern.

Remember, the first card goes to the bottom of the facedown pile, the second card goes faceup on the table, the third card goes to the bottom, the fourth card goes faceup, etc., until all seven are on the table.

What is the beginning arrangement of the cards?

10

Mary has placed two chocolate cupcakes in one drawer of her kitchen. In another drawer, she has placed a chocolate and a vanilla cupcake; and in a third drawer, two vanilla cupcakes. Her brother knows the arrangement of the cupcakes, but doesn't know which drawers contain each arrangement.

Mary opens one of the drawers, pulls out a chocolate cupcake, and says to her brother, "If you can tell me what the chances are that the other cupcake in this drawer is chocolate, I'll let you have any cupcake you like."

What are the chances that the other cupcake is chocolate?

11

A team of cryptologists is in the process of developing a four-digit code that can never be broken. They know that if the code begins with 0, 5, or 7, it can be cracked. What is the greatest number of four-digit codes the team can use that won't be broken?

12

What word can be added to the end of each of the following words to form new words?

MOON

SHOE

MONKEY

13

If 7^{33} is divided by 10, what will the remainder be? You may get the wrong answer if you try to solve this on some calculators.

14

If the first three of the following statements are true, is the conclusion true or false?

All Nebraskans are Cornhusker fans.
Some Cornhusker fans are also Hawkeye fans.
Some Hawkeye fans are also Cyclone fans.
Therefore, some Nebraskans are Cyclone fans.

15

In a strange, distant land, they have a slightly different number system than ours. For instance, $4 \times 6 = 30$ and $4 \times 7 = 34$. Based on this, what is the value of $5 \times 4 \times 7$ in this land? Hint: Remember this is a number *system*.

16

Ann, Boobie, Cathy, and Dave are at their monthly business meeting. Their occupations are author, biologist, chemist, and doctor, but not necessarily in that order. Dave just told the biologist that Cathy was on her way with doughnuts. Ann is sitting across from the doctor and next to the chemist. The doctor was thinking that Boobie was a goofy name for parents to choose, but didn't say anything.

What is each person's occupation?

17

See if you can establish a pattern to fill in the fourth grid in this sequence puzzle.

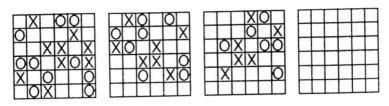

18

The sum of the infinite series ½ + ¼ + ⅛ + 1/16 . . . equals 1. What is the sum of the infinite series ¼ + 1/16 + 1/64 + 1/256 . . . ?

19

This puzzle requires analytical reasoning. Determine the relationships between the figures and words to find two solutions.

○○○ = LAG   RAB = ○
                          ○

◇ ◇ = LEB

◇ ◇ ◇ = ?   REG = ◇
                          ◇
                          ◇

REBRAG = ?

20

Here's another opportunity to use analytical reasoning, but this puzzle has a slightly different twist.

In a foreign language:

"*Kaf navcki roi*" means "Take three pieces."

"*Kir roi palt*" means "Hide three coins."

"*Inoti kaf kir*" means "Cautiously take coins."

How would you say "Hide pieces cautiously" in this language?

21

Seventy-eight percent of all people are gum chewers, and thirty-five percent of all people are under the age of fifteen. Given that a person has been selected at random, what is the probability that the person is not a gum chewer and above age fifteen?

35 %   100 % 65 %
5 %
30 %   65
         22
         130
         130
         1430

22

What is the next letter in this series?

A   B   D   O   P   Q   ?

1   1   2

23

A. 2^{65}

B. $(2^{64} + 2^{63} + 2^{62} \ldots 2^2 + 2^1 + 2^0)$

In comparing the values of A and B, which of these statements is correct?

B is 2^{64} larger than A.
A is 2^{64} larger than B.
A and B are equal.
B is larger than A by 1.
A is larger than B by 1.

24

Classic puzzles are fun to revisit now and then, especially if there's a new twist.

In this puzzle, see if you can be as successful as John in retrieving water for his mother. The new twist? The buckets are different sizes.

John's mother told him to go to the river and bring back exactly 9 gallons of water in one trip. She gave him a six-gallon bucket and a five-gallon bucket to complete his task. Of course, John's mother told him she'd bake his favorite cake if he came back with the 9 gallons.

John had his cake and ate it, too. Can you?

25

1881 : 1961 :: 6009 : ?

26

In the world of physics, sometimes things that appear to move forward are actually moving backward. Knowing this, can you complete this analogy?

EMIT : STAR :: TIME : ?

27

What is the next number in this series?

1   9   18   25   27   21   ?

28

Nine men and seven women pick as much corn in five days as seven men and eleven women pick in four days. Who are the better corn pickers and by how much?

29

Puzzles 29 to 35 are all composed of numbers, but that doesn't necessarily mean that the numbers contained in any given problem are mathematically related. Your mind will have to be flexible to determine what type of relationship the numbers in the series have with each other. There are no holds barred, and each puzzle may have a solution more obvious than you realize at first.

What is the next number in this series?

1   2   4   13   31   112   ?

30

What is the next number in this series?

1 4 2 8 5 7 ?

Hint: This might be just a fraction of what you think.

31

What is the missing number in this series?

9 3 15 7 12 ? 13 5 17 11

32

What is the next number in this series?

0 2 4 6 8 12 12 20 16 ?

33

What is the missing number in this series?

16 21 26 26 12 ? 19

34

What is the next number in this series?

3 4 11 16 27 36 ?

35

What is the next number in this series?

224 1 8 30 5 ?

36

No puzzle book would be complete without at least one anagram. Here is a phrase that, when unscrambled, spells the name of a famous person. The phrase gives a small hint relating to the person's identity.

BEEN IN STAR LITE

37

Imagine a 3 × 3 × 3-inch opaque cube divided into twenty-seven 1-inch cubes. Quickly, what are the maximum number of 1-inch cubes that can be seen by one person from any point in space?

38

What are the values of §, $\otimes$, and ¶?

§ + § + § + $\otimes$ = § + § + $\otimes$ + $\otimes$ + $\otimes$ = ¶ + ¶

$$¶ - § = 6$$

39

Below are four grids. See if you can determine the logic used in arriving at each successive grid. What would the next grid look like?

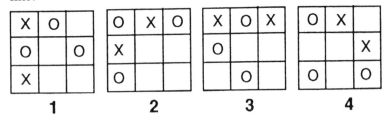

1   **2**   **3**   **4**

40

Bill is standing on the ground, looking directly at one of the faces of a new museum built in the shape of a four-sided pyramid. All the sides are identical.

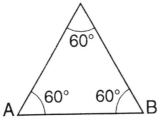

At night, each edge of the pyramid is illuminated with an array of colored lights. Bill's friend Judy is in an airplane touring the area. When her plane, which is several thousand feet high, flies directly over the top of the pyramid, Bill asks her, via walkie-talkie, if she can tell what angle lines A and B make at the peak of the pyramid. Judy answers without hesitation, but it's not what Bill expected. Why?

41

Nitram Rendrag, the world's most renowned puzzle creator, often rents a private dining car on the Charlotte–Greensboro–Charlotte turn-around shuttle. The railroad charges Rendrag $120 for the trip. On a recent trip, the conductor informed Rendrag that there were two students at the Franklin station who wished to go from Franklin to Greensboro and back to Franklin. Franklin is halfway between Charlotte and Greensboro. Rendrag asked the conductor to let the students ride with him.

When the students boarded Rendrag's car, he said, "If you can tell me the mathematically correct price you should pay for your portion of the trip, I'll let you ride for free. Remember, your answer has to be mathematically equitable for all of us." How much should the students pay for their journey?

42

Of the four choices below, which best completes this figure analogy?

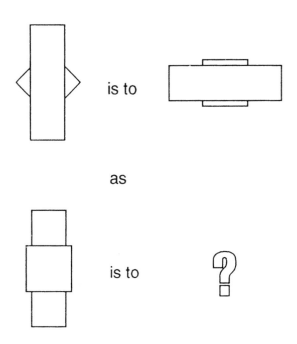

is to

as

is to

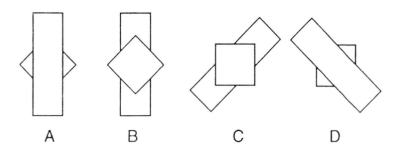

A B C D

43

Of the four choices below, which best completes this figure analogy?

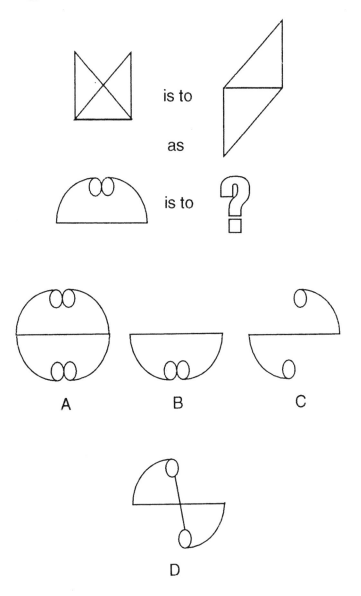

A

B

C

D

44

Which of the five choices completes this analogy?

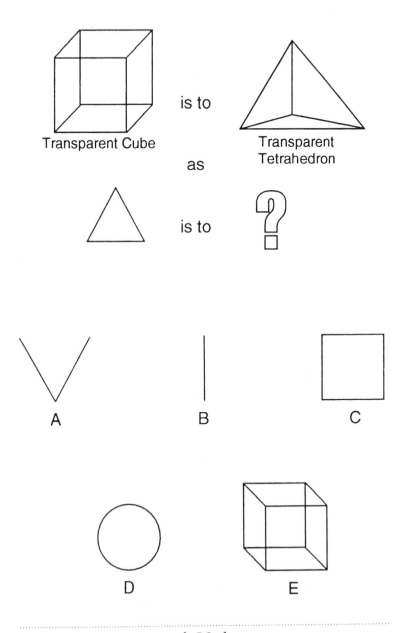

Transparent Cube **is to** Transparent Tetrahedron

as

is to ?

A

B

C

D

E

45

Complete this analogy.

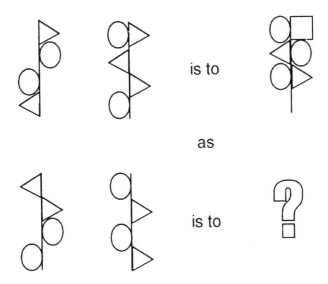

is to

as

is to

46

Which one of the following figures does not belong? Hint: Don't consider symmetry.

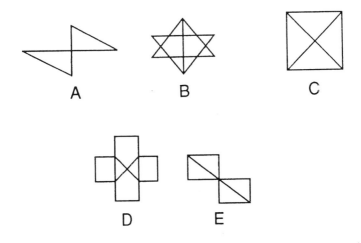

A   B   C

D   E

47

A northbound freight train with 100 boxcars will soon meet a southbound freight train with 100 boxcars in single-track territory. They'll meet near a siding track that has a maximum capacity of 80 boxcars. The engines of the southbound train are too heavy to enter any portion of the siding trackage.

With the following information, is it possible for the two trains to get around each other and continue on their trip in the same direction as they started? If so, how?

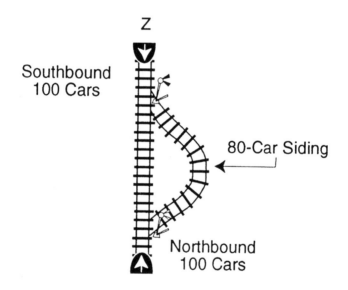

Basic RR Rules

No cars may roll freely by themselves.
All cars and engines have couplers on both ends.

The siding track has switches on both ends.
Engines can move in either direction.
Both trains have radio communications and cabooses.

48

Find the hidden phrase or title.

49

Find the hidden phrase or title.

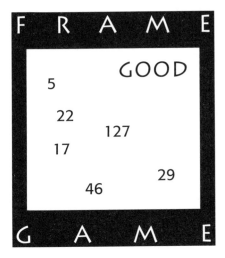

50

A well-known puzzle asks how many revolutions a rotating coin can make around a duplicate fixed coin in one full rotation. The answer is two. This is a variation of that puzzle, and you may be surprised at the answer.

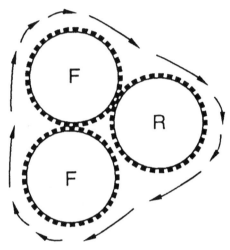

A rotating gear in a diesel engine revolves around two fixed gears and looks like this.

All three gears are identical in size. How many revolutions will Gear R make in one full rotation around the fixed gears?

51

Sara rows down the Snake River at a rate of 4 m.p.h. with the current. After she's traveled for two hours, she turns around and rows back against the current to where she started. It takes her four hours to return. What is Sara's rowing rate in still water? What is the rate of the Snake River?

52

Candace is Jane's daughter's aunt's husband's daughter's sister. What is the relationship between Candace and Jane?

53

English puzzler Henry Dudeney was a master at creating all types of intriguing train puzzles. From the speeds of roaring locomotives to the times on station clocks, his train puzzles demonstrated elegant simplicity while testing the solver's deductive reasoning power.

In keeping with the spirit of Dudeney's train puzzles, Professor Fractal was taking his best math-prize student to Kensington Station to board a train for Leeds, for the British Isles Math Contest. As they entered the depot, the station clock chimed six o'clock. The professor turned to his math whiz and said, "If you can tell me at what time, immediately prior to six o'clock, the hands of the clock were exactly opposite each other, I'll buy you dinner before your departure."

The student enjoyed a delicious London broil. What was the exact time in hours, minutes, and seconds when the hands of the clock were opposite each other, immediately prior to six o'clock?

54

See if you can deduce the logic of the letters in and around the circles to determine what the missing letter is inside the last circle.

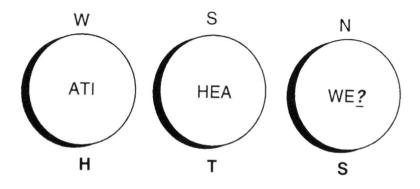

What's the missing number?

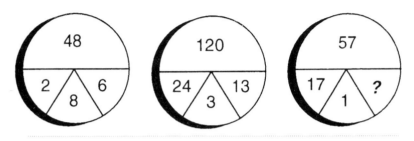

If one type of weight can balance either 5 gold coins or 4 silver coins, then ten weights of the same type can balance 20 gold coins and how many silver coins in the same scale pan?

Sometimes in school or business, we are given information that looks impossible to decipher, only to find out that applying a little "elbow grease" aids in sorting things out. Below are several statements that attempt to form some relationships between the letters A, B, C, and D, and the numbers 1, 2, 3, and 4. Using the following information, see if you can straighten out this confusion and identify each letter with its associated number.

If A is 1, then B is not 3.
If B is not 1, then D is 4.
If B is 1, then C is 4.
If C is 3, then D is not 2.
If C is not 2, then D is 2.
If D is 3, then A is not 4.

Hint: Make a grid with A, B, C, and D on one side and 1, 2, 3, and 4 on the other. Then make some assumptions.

58

Linda wants to drain the water out of a 55-gallon barrel. She has the choice of using either a 2-inch-diameter hose or two 1-inch-diameter hoses to drain the barrel. Which will drain the barrel faster—the 2-inch hose or the two 1-inch hoses? Will they drain the water equally fast?

59

It seems that every puzzle writer has a friend who is a brilliant logician and who makes a living solving impossible problems for the government or tracking down criminals.

Molly O'Coley is of that rare breed. The 'Mazin' Ms. Molly, as she's known to Scotland Yard, sent me a note some time ago about a notorious international criminal who was jailed due to her efforts. Much secrecy had surrounded the trial because the prosecution didn't want the public to know the large sum of money recovered by Ms. Molly. They felt that information might hinder future efforts to bring the criminal's associates to trial.

Below is the total contents of Ms. Molly's note to me. Each letter of this note stands for a number, and the total is the sum that Ms. Molly recovered. Can you find the exact amount?

$$\begin{array}{r} T R A I L \\ + T R I A L \\ \hline G U I L T Y \end{array}$$

Y = 3

Note: The letter Y is not part of the addition problem. I later discovered that the Y = 3 also indicated the number of associates the criminal had. Ms. Molly found them in Stuttgart and had them extradited to London.

60

In this alphametic, if you find that one of the letters is equal to nine, then another letter must equal 5 and still another must be 4. Let E = 4 and V = 7.

$$
\begin{array}{r}
\text{A} \quad \text{F I V E} \\
+ \text{A} \quad \text{F O U R} \\
\hline
\text{I F} \quad \text{N I N E}
\end{array}
$$

61

After trying several times to reach my wife by phone and failing, due to problems with the telephone, I arrived home to find this curious coded message left next to the telephone. Can you decipher my wife's message?

9368 86 289 2 639 74663

62

There are 100 students applying for summer jobs in a university's geology/geography department. Ten of the students have never taken a course in geology or geography. Sixty-three of the students have taken at least one geology course. Eighty-one have taken at least one geography course.

What is the probability that of the 100 applicants any student selected at random has taken either geography or geology, but not both?

How many students have taken at least one course in both geology and geography?

63

Find the hidden phrase or title.

64

Here's another old puzzle with a different twist. Two friends were talking, and the first one said, "Do you remember the brainteaser about a drawer full of black and blue socks?" His friend replied he wasn't sure. "The object is to determine the minimum number of socks you'd have to pick in the dark in order to have a pair of the same color," said the first friend. "Yes," said the second friend, "I remember. The answer is three." "That's right," replied the storyteller. "Quickly now, tell me the minimum number of socks you'd need to take from the drawer if it contained twenty-four blue socks and twenty black socks and you wanted to be assured of a pair of black socks?"

65

(17:8) : (25:7) :: (32:5) : (_?_ : _?_)

66

Find the hidden phrase or title.

67

At a gathering of mathematicians, everyone shook hands with four other people, except for two people, who shook hands with only one other person (not each other).

If one person shakes hands with another, each person counts as one handshake.

What is the minimum number of people who could have been present? What is the total number of handshakes that took place?

68

You've just thrown your first two dice in a craps game and your point is 10. This means that you must continue to roll the dice until you roll another 10 to make your point. If you roll a 7 before you roll another 10, you lose.

What are your chances of winning with 10 as your point?

69

The numbers 1 through 6 are arranged so that any number resting between and below two other numbers is the difference between those two numbers.

Using numbers 1 through 10, fill in the X's below to create a "difference triangle" with the same conditions. If you'd like a little stiffer challenge, try this using the numbers 1 through 15 in five rows.

70

This puzzle is a variation of the game nim, named by Harvard mathematics professor Charles Bouton in 1901. Mathemagician Martin Gardner discusses a version of the game in his book *Entertaining Mathematical Puzzles*.

In Gardner's version, coins are arranged like this:

Two players take turns removing the coins. More than one coin can be removed on a turn as long as they are in the same row. The person who is forced to take the last coin is the loser. Gardner asks the reader if an ironclad winning first move can be determined. The answer is yes. The first player removes three coins from the bottom row.

In our version of nim, an extra coin is added to the top so that the ten coins are arranged like this.

The rules are basically the same, except that in our game, if more than one coin is removed from any row, the coins must be adjacent to each other. For example, if a coin had been removed from the bottom row by a player, the other player may *not* pick up the remaining three coins.

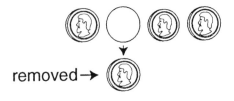

In this case, the second player may pick up the coin on the left or either or both on the right. In our version, there are two winning first moves. What are they?

71

Logician George Summers's puzzles are among the best. His logic brainteasers offer a clear, straightforward presentation of the puzzle, yet fully test the deductive reasoning process of even the best puzzle enthusiasts. His book *The Great Book of Mind Teasers & Mind Puzzlers* will keep you busy for days.

In one of his creations, which could be called the "letter cross," letters represent numbers, and you must make several deductions to come up with the value of each letter.

Here is a version of a letter cross puzzle. Although not particularly difficult, it still requires several steps for its solution. Solve this, and you'll be ready to tackle some of Summers's crunchers.

$$\begin{array}{cccc} A & B & C & D \\ & & & E \\ & & & F \\ G & H & I & J \end{array}$$

$$A + B + C + D = D + E + F + G = G + H + I + J = 17$$

$A = 4$ and $J = 0$. Using all digits from 0 through 9 only once, find the values for B, C, D, E, F, and G.

There is more than one correct answer. Several numbers are interchangeable.

72

Here's a punchy clue to a series question.

Cubes and squares can be one and the same,
But if this so happens, they need a new name.
Squbes sounds OK, so I'll leave it at that,
But can you now tell me where the next one is at?

$$64 \quad 729 \quad 4{,}096 \quad 15{,}625 \quad \underline{\ ?\ }$$

73

There are five boxes such that Box C fits into Box A, Box D fits into Box B or Box C, and Box A is not the largest.

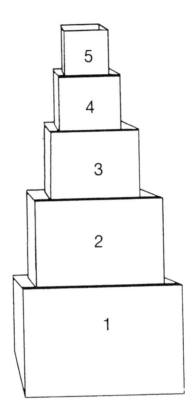

As you can see, Box 1 is the largest and each progressive box is smaller, so that Box 5 is the smallest. The number of the box that represents Box A plus the number of the box that represents Box E is equal to the number of the box that represents Box D plus the number of the box that represents Box C. Determine the size of Boxes A through E from largest to smallest.

74

Three identical bags contain colored balls. Each bag has one red and one white ball. A ball is drawn out of Bag 1, another out of Bag 2, and another out of Bag 3.

What are the chances that you'll end up with exactly 2 white balls?

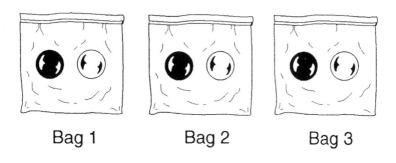

Bag 1   Bag 2   Bag 3

75

Three straight cuts on a single plane through a cube will result in a maximum of eight pieces. What is the maximum number of pieces that will result when four planar cuts are made through a cube? The slices may not be rearranged between cuts.

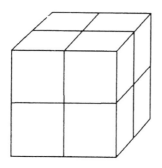

76

Take three coins and arrange them like this.

Now, if you wanted to turn the triangle upside down using the minimum number of moves, you would move Coin 1 below Coins 2 and 3 like this.

What is the minimum number of coins you need to move to turn the following triangle upside down?

Can you find a general pattern or formula for predicting how many coins you must move to turn any triangle of N length upside down?

77

This game, often called the triangle pegboard game, has been around a long time and offers a good challenge. Maybe you've seen it in restaurants throughout the country.

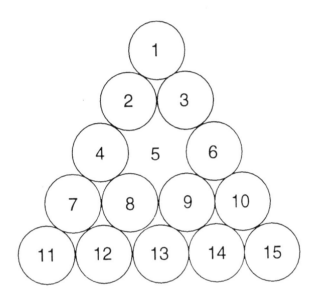

The object of the game, which can also be played with coins, is to jump one peg over another, staying inside the triangle. After jumping over a peg, remove that peg. The goal is to end up with only one peg. Begin with 14 pegs or coins and leave the middle hole open. There is only one solution (two if you count its mirror image). If you've tried this puzzle, you know that it can drive you crazy if you get off on the wrong track.

On the next page are the first six moves towards the correct solution. Of course, if you want to go it alone, stop reading here.

Take fourteen markers or coins and arrange them as shown. Don't forget to remove a marker after you've jumped over it.

Here's your start.

> Step 1—Move 12 to 5.
> Step 2—Move 10 to 8.
> Step 3—Move 14 to 12.
> Step 4—Move 3 to 10.
> Step 5—Move 2 to 9.
> Step 6—Move 7 to 2.

There are thirteen jumps in all. The remaining seven moves are in the Answers section.

78

Imagine that you must build a tunnel through eight identical cubes. The tunnel must be continuous and start from any of the three exposed faces of Cube 1. The tunnel has to pass through each of the eight cubes only once, and it cannot cut through any place where more than two cubes meet. How many cubes must be excluded as the tunnel's final or exit cube? What are their numbers?

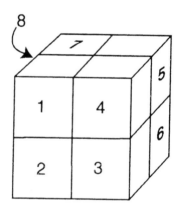

79

Below are five different sides of a solid object constructed out of several identical cubes fused together. What does the sixth side look like?

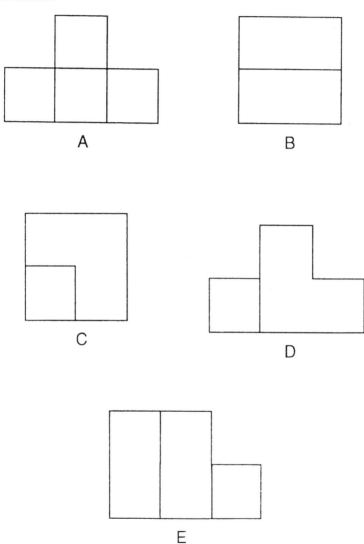

A

B

C

D

E

80

Find the hidden phrase or title.

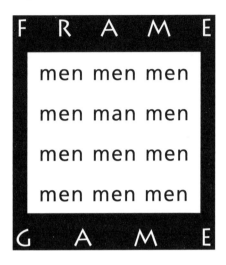

81

Arrange twelve toothpicks into a sort of window pane. Rearrange only three of them to create ten different triangles of any size.

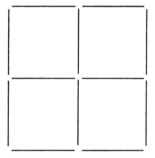

82

Find the hidden phrase or title.

83

Four friends, Bob, Bill, Pat, and Tom, are nicknamed Rabbit, Walleye, Fly, and Bear—but not necessarily in that order.

a. Pat can run faster than Rabbit, but can't lift as much weight as Fly.

b. Rabbit is stronger than Tom, but slower than Walleye.

c. Bob is faster than both Pat and Bear, but not as strong as Rabbit.

What is the nickname of each friend?

84

A certain blend of grass seed is made by mixing Brand A at $9.00 a pound with Brand B at $4.00 a pound. If the blend is worth $7.00 a pound, how many pounds of Brand A are needed to make 40 pounds of the blend?

85

Two rockets are launched simultaneously from two different positions.

Rocket A will land at the same spot from which Rocket B was launched, and Rocket B will land at the same spot where Rocket A was launched, allowing a small distance to the left or right to avoid a midair collision.

The rockets are launched from the same angle, and therefore travel the same distance both vertically and horizontally. If the rockets reach their destinations in one and nine hours, respectively, after passing each another, how much faster is one rocket than the other?

A   B

86

Your chemistry teacher asks you to convert temperatures from one system of measurement to another. These are new systems for determining temperatures, so the classic conversions from Centigrade, Fahrenheit, and Kelvin don't apply.

You are told that 14° in the first system is equal to 36° in the second system. You also know that 133° in the first system is equal to 87° in the second.

What is the method or formula for converting one system to the other?

At what temperature will both thermometers read the same?

87

Here is a sequence of five figures. What would the sixth figure look like?

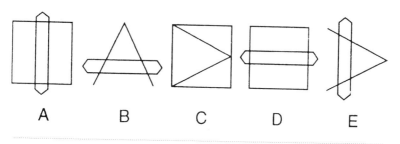

A   B   C   D   E

88

One of these figures doesn't belong with the rest. Don't be concerned about symmetry. Which doesn't belong? Why?

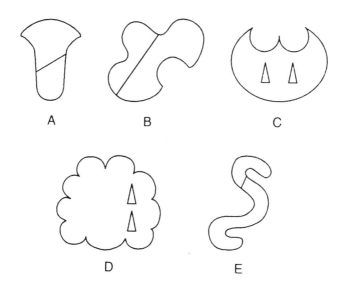

A   B   C

D   E

89

Apollona Constantino has 57 of them. Maggie Lieber has 36 of them. Paul Furstenburg has 45 of them. Based on the above, how many of them does Mary Les have?

90

How many individual cubes are in this configuration? All rows and columns in the figure are complete unless you actually see them end.

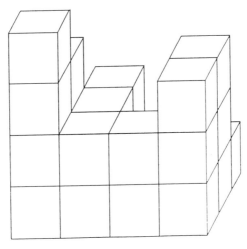

91

Thirteen boys and girls wait to take their seats in the same row in a movie theater. The row is thirteen seats long. They decide that after the first person sits down, the next person has to sit next to the first. The third sits next to one of the first two and so on until all thirteen are seated. In other words, no person except the first can take a seat with empty seats on both sides.

How many different ways can this be accomplished, assuming that the first person can choose any of the thirteen seats?

92

Three dollar bills were exchanged for a certain number of nickels and the same number of dimes. How many nickels were there? Read this puzzle to a group of friends and see how long it takes to come up with the answer. You may be surprised!

93

In the multiplication puzzle below, x, y, and z represent different digits. What is the sum of x, y, and z?

$$\begin{array}{r} yx \\ \times\ 7 \\ \hline zxx \end{array}$$

94

Alex, Ryan, and Steven are sports fans. Each has a different favorite sport among football, baseball, and basketball. Alex does not like basketball; Steven does not like basketball or baseball. Name each person's favorite sport.

95

Let's say 26 zips weigh as much as 4 crids and 2 wobs. Also, 8 zips and 2 crids have the same weight as 2 wobs. How many zips have the weight of 1 wob?

96

Find the hidden phrase or title.

97

There is a certain logic shared by the following four circles. Can you determine the missing number in the last circle?

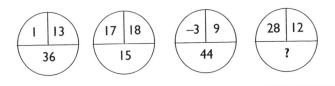

98

What is ½ of ⅔ of ⅗ of 240 divided by ½?

99

Find the hidden phrase or title.

100

The three words below can be rearranged into two words that are also three words! Can you decipher this curious puzzle?

the red rows

101

Can you determine the next letter in the following series?

A   C   F   H   K   M   ?

102

One of the figures below lacks a common characteristic that the other five figures have. Which one is it and why?

Hint: This does not have to do with right angles or symmetry.

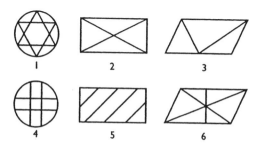

103

Find the hidden phrase or title.

104

A car travels from point A to point B (a distance of one mile) at 30 miles per hour. How fast would the car have to travel from point B to point C (also a distance of one mile) to average 60 miles per hour for the entire trip?

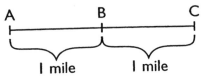

105

Try your luck at this "trickle-down" puzzle. Starting at the top, change one letter of each succeeding word to arrive at the word at the bottom.

106

If the length of a rectangle is increased by 25 percent and its width is decreased by 25 percent, what is the percentage of change in its area?

107

A friend has a bag containing two cherry gumdrops and one orange gumdrop. She offers to give you all the gumdrops you want if you can tell her the chances of drawing a cherry gumdrop on the first draw and the orange gumdrop on the second draw. Can you meet your friend's challenge?

108

The design on the left is made up of three paper squares of different sizes, one on top of the other. What is the minimum number of squares needed to create the design on the right?

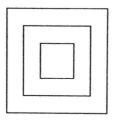 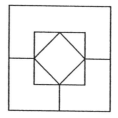

109

Here's a variation on an old classic. On what side of the line does the "R" go?

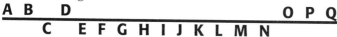

A B   D   O P Q
   C   E F G H I J K L M N

110

Find the hidden phrase or title.

111

Given the initial letters of the missing words, complete this sentence.

There are 100 Y in a C.

112

If I tripled one-quarter of a fraction and multiplied it by that fraction, I would get one-twelfth. What is the original fraction?

113

Two toy rockets are heading directly for each other. One is traveling at 50 miles per hour and the other is traveling at 70 miles per hour. How far apart will these two rockets be one minute before they collide?

114

Find the hidden phrase or title.

115

Think of five squares that are the same size. In how many ways can these five squares be combined, edge to edge? (No mirror images allowed.)

116

What number is four times one-third the number that is one-sixteenth less than three-thirty-seconds?

117

Below are five words. By adding the same three letters at the beginning of each word, you can come up with five new words. What three letters will do the trick?

HER
ION
OR
IF
TO

118

If x^2 is larger than 9, which of the following is true?

    a. x is greater than 0.
    b. 0 is greater than x.
    c. x is equal to 0.
    d. x^3 is greater than 0.
    e. There is insufficient information to determine a solution.

119

Based on the following information, how many pleezorns does Ahmad Adziz have?

        Molly O'Brien has 22 pleezorns.
        Debbie Reynolds has 28 pleezorns.
        Roberto Montgomery has 34 pleezorns.

120

What is 10 percent of 90 percent of 80 percent?

121

Find the hidden phrase or title.

122

A mixture of chemicals costs $40 per ton. It is composed of one type of chemical that costs $48 per ton and another type of chemical that costs $36 per ton. In what ratio were these chemicals mixed?

123

Find the hidden phrase or title.

124

How many triangles of any size are in the figure below?

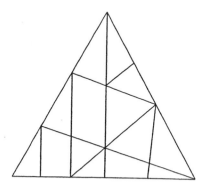

125

If the ratio of 5*x* to 4*y* is 7 to 8, what is the ratio of 10*x* to 14*y*?

126

Decipher the following cryptogram:

WLA'P XLJAP RLJO XGMXBSAE NSQLOS PGSR GCPXG.

127

Find the hidden phrase or title.

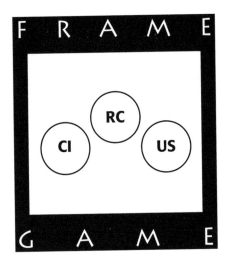

128

How many four-letter words can you find in the word "twinkle"? (Try for at least 15.)

129

Do this quickly: Write down twelve thousand twelve hundred twenty-two.

130

Below are four sets of letters that are related in a way known to virtually everyone. Can you find the missing two letters? (*Hint:* Some people have been known to take months to solve this!)

ON
DJ
FM
AM
? ?

131

Find the hidden phrase or title.

132

Find the hidden phrase or title.

133

In the strange land of Doubledown the alphabet appears to be hieroglyphics, but it isn't really much different from ours. Below is one of the Doubledown months spelled out. Which month of ours is comparable?

134

Which is larger, $3^7 + 7^3$ or the sum of $4^6 + 6^4$? No calculators, please.

135

Unscramble this word:

GORNSIMMAROCI

136

Given the initial letters of the missing words, complete this sentence.

There is one W on a U.

137

Below are six rays. Choosing two of the rays, how many angles of less than 90 degrees can you form? (Angle ACB is less than 90 degrees.)

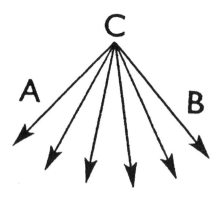

138

By arranging all nine integers in a certain order, it is possible to come up with fractions equal to ½, ⅓, ¼, ⅕, ⅙, ⅐, ⅛, and ⅑. See if you can come up with one of these.

Example: $\frac{1}{8} = \frac{3,187}{25,496}$

139

Find the hidden phrase or title.

140

What are the two missing numbers in the series below?

8, 15, 10, 13, 12, 11, 14, 9, 16, 7, ?, ?

141

What is the value of **z** in the following problem? (Each number is a positive integer between 0 and 9.)

$$x$$
$$y$$
$$+z$$
$$\overline{xy}$$

142

Referring back to the last puzzle, where **z** was found to be 9, what is the value of **x**?

$$\begin{array}{r} x \\ y \\ +z \\ \hline xy \end{array}$$

143

Most of us know the following rules of divisibility:

A number is divisible by 2 if it ends in an even digit.

A number is divisible by 3 if the sum of its digits is divisible by 3.

Is there such a rule for dividing by 8?

144

Which one of the following five words doesn't belong with the others, and why?

Pail
Skillet
Knife
Suitcase
Doorbell

145

If you wrote down all the numbers from 5 to 83, how many times would you write the number 4?

146

Four of the figures below share a characteristic that the fifth figure doesn't have. Can you determine which figure doesn't go with the others and why?

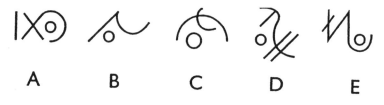

| A | B | C | D | E |

147

Find the hidden phrase or title.

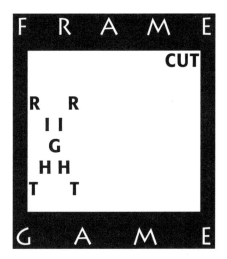

148

A certain barrel of candy can be equally divided (without cutting pieces) between five, seven, or thirteen people. What is the least number of pieces of candy the barrel could contain?

149

Find the hidden phrase or title.

150

Which is greater, 107 percent of 300 or 50 percent of 600?

151

What is the value of the following?

$$\frac{1}{3 + \dfrac{1}{3\frac{1}{3}}}$$

152

The diagram below is the beginning of a "magic square" in which all rows and columns and both diagonals add up to 34. Can you fill in the rest of the numbers?

1	8	13	12
14			
4		16	
15			

153

The diagram below can be drawn without lifting your pencil or crossing any other line. Can you do it?

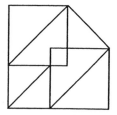

154

Imagine that a coin called a "kookla" is equal in value to either 7 gold pieces or 13 silver pieces. If you have 40 kooklas that you want to exchange for both silver and gold pieces and your bank has only 161 gold pieces on hand, how many silver pieces should you expect to receive with the 161 gold pieces?

155

The two numbers in each box have the same relationship to each other as do the two numbers in every other box. What is the missing number?

| 3, 8 | −5, 24 | 0, −1 | 9, 80 | 6, ? |

156

There are six chairs, each of a different color. In how many different ways can these six chairs be arranged in a straight line?

157

Find the hidden phrase or title.

158

Do the numbers 9 and 10 go above or below the line?

```
1     2                          6
3     4     5              7     8
```

159

Find the hidden phrase or title.

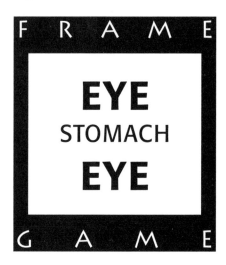

160

A concept that math students often find difficult to understand is that a negative multiplied by a negative results in a positive (example: –5 × –5 = 25). Can you come up with a real-life example, in words, to illustrate this?

161

Unscramble the following word:

RGAALEB

162

Without using + or − signs, arrange five 8s so that they equal 9.

163

How many individual cubes are in the configuration below? (All rows and columns run to completion unless you see them end.)

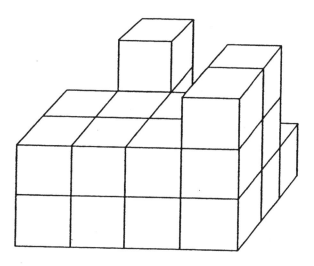

164

How many different words can you make from the word "Thanksgiving"? You might be surprised to find how many new words can be made from a word that doesn't contain the letter "e."

165

What is ¹⁄₁₀ divided by ½ divided by ¹⁄₅ times ⁷⁄₉?

Find the hidden phrase or title.

167

When the proper weights are assigned, this mobile is perfectly balanced. Can you determine the three missing weights?

(*Hint:* Try starting with the 8-foot section of the mobile. Remember that Distance × Weight = Distance × Weight.)

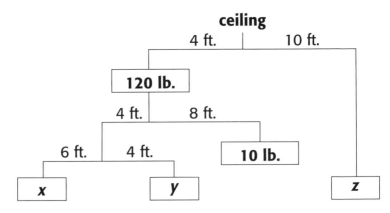

168

Below are two numbers represented by **x** and **y**. Regardless of the values of **x** and **y**, all possible answers resulting from the difference in these two numbers share one unique characteristic. What is it?

$$xy$$
$$- \underline{yx}$$
$$??$$

169

The perimeter of a square has a value that is two-thirds of the number representing its square footage. What is the size of the square?

170

Find the hidden phrase or title.

171

In the game of craps, what are the chances that you will be a winner on your first roll by getting either a 7 or an 11?

172

Find the hidden phrase or title.

173

Here's another four-letter "trickle-down" puzzle. Find the three missing words, each with only one letter changed from the previous word, to arrive at **BARN**.

174

What is the value of T in the following puzzle?

$$A + B = H$$
$$H + P = T$$
$$T + A = F$$
$$B + P + F = 30$$
$$A = 2$$

175

If five potatoes and six onions cost $1.22 and six potatoes and five onions cost $1.31, what does an onion cost?

176

Find the hidden phrase or title.

177

Below are 10 matchsticks of equal length. By moving 2 and only 2 matchsticks, can you create 2 squares only, with no leftover matchsticks?

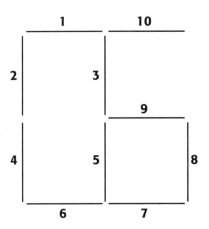

178

A bag contains 7 green balls and 3 red ones. What is the probability of randomly taking out 3 green balls in succession without looking if:

A: Each ball is replaced before the next draw?

B: The balls are not replaced?

179

Find the missing number in the following series:

$$20/48 \quad 1/3 \quad 1/4 \quad 1/6 \quad 1/12 \quad ?$$

180

Find the hidden phrase or title.

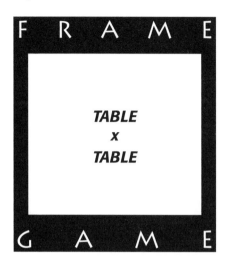

181

Given the initial letters of the missing words, complete this sentence.

There are 206 B in the H B.

182

What is the first number having factors that add up to more than the number itself? (Don't include the number itself as one of the factors.)

183

What number is ¼ of ⅓ of ⅙ of 432, divided by ⅓?

184

Find the hidden phrase or title.

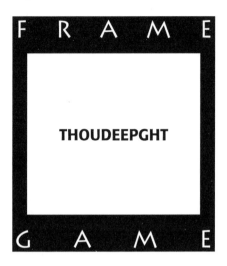

185

One hundred people are applying for a sales position that would require them to sell both golf equipment and athletic shoes. Thirteen of the applicants have no prior experience in sales. Sixty-five of the applicants have previously sold golf equipment, and 78 of the applicants have sold athletic shoes. How many of the applicants have experience in selling both golf equipment and athletic shoes?

186

What's the difference between 11 yards square and 11 square yards?

187

Find the four-letter word that will make new words when added in front of these:

GUARD
LONG
TIME

Find the hidden phrase or title.

189

What is the first year after the year 2000 in which the numbers of the year will read the same right-side-up and upside-down? What is the second year in which this will occur? (No fair using digital numerals, like 2!)

190

H is to one as C is to six as N is to ?

191

Find the hidden phrase or title.

192

A "perfect" number is a number whose factors add up to the number (not including the number itself). For example:

The factors of 6 are 3, 2, and 1 and 3 + 2 + 1 = 6.

The factors of 28 are 14, 7, 4, 2, and 1 and 14 + 7 + 4 + 2 + 1 = 28.

What are the next two perfect numbers?

193

What are the chances of flipping a penny four times and getting at least two tails?

194

Find the hidden phrase or title.

195

Decipher the following cryptogram. Each letter represents another letter in the alphabet.

OTD X GACOT ST BPWF WASFTOOX.

196

What is the next number in the following series?

**1, 2, 6, 30, 60, 180, 900,
1,800, 5,400, _____**

197

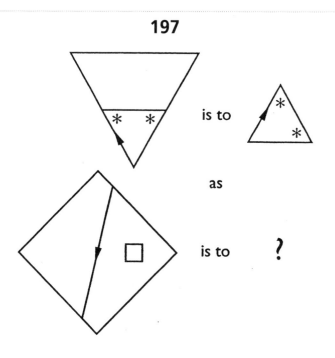

is to

as

is to **?**

198

A pipe can fill a swimming pool in three hours. A second pipe can fill the pool in two hours. If both pipes are turned on at the same time, how long will it take them to fill the pool?

199

I am ten years older than my sister. There was a time when I was three times older than she was, and in one year I will be twice as old as she is. What is my age now?

200

Here's an interesting twist on an old series puzzle. See if you can come up with the missing letter. (*Hint:* This problem is best approached with an even hand.)

T   F   S   E   T   T   F   ?

201

Find the hidden phrase or title.

202

Susie's and Sally's last names are Billingsley and Jenkins, but not necessarily in that order. Two of the following statements are false. What is the real name of each person?

Susie's last name is Billingsley.
Susie's last name is Jenkins.
Sally's last name is Jenkins.

203

Can you come up with a quick way to find the square of 95 mentally . . . or for that matter the square of 45, 55, 65, etc.?

Hint: Think of square numbers above and below each of these numbers.

There is more than one way to do this.

204

If you find the correct starting point in the wheel below and move either clockwise or counterclockwise, the letters will spell out a common everyday word. What is the missing letter, and what is the word?

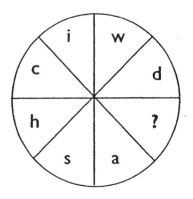

205

Find the hidden phrase or title.

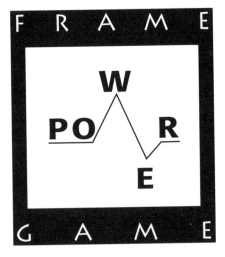

206

How many digits must be changed in the following addition problem to make the sum equal 245?

$$
\begin{array}{r}
8\,9 \\
1\,6 \\
+\quad 9\,8 \\
\hline
\end{array}
$$

207

In a certain box of candy, the number of caramels is 25 percent of the number of other candies in the box. What percentage of the entire box are the caramels?

208

Find the hidden phrase or title.

209

Given the initial letters of the missing words, complete the following sentence. (*Hint:* Think of hydrogen.)

There are 118 E in the P T.

210

Change one and only one letter in each successive word to come up with the next word:

R O A D

———————

———————

———————

L O O P

211

One of the following diagrams doesn't fit with the others. Which one is it? Why? *Hint:* Think symmetry.

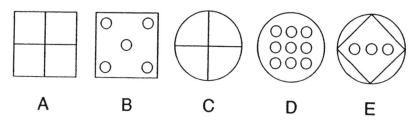

A   B   C   D   E

212

Here's fun with roman numerals. See if you can match column A to column B.

$\overline{V}$	100
$\overline{M}$	500
$\overline{C}$	1,000
C	5,000
$\overline{L}$	10,000
X	50,000
$\overline{D}$	100,000
D	500,000
M	1,000,000

213

Find the hidden phrase or title.

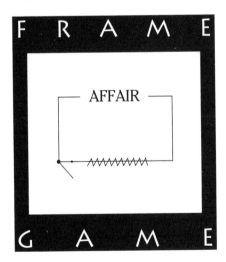

214

Using only the letters of the top row on a typewriter, how many 10-letter words can you create?
Remember, the letters are

QWERTYUIOP

215

Find the hidden phrase or title.

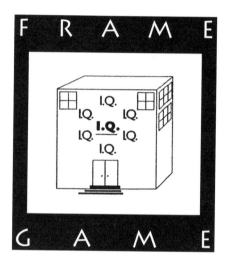

216

In a certain game, a ball can fall through any of 50 holes evenly spaced around a wheel. The chance that a ball would fall into any one particular hole is 1 in 50. What are the chances that 2 balls circling the wheel at the same time would fall into the same hole?

217

What is the missing number in the following series?

84   12   2   ²/₅   ¹/₁₀   ?

218

Find the hidden phrase or title.

219

A man spent three-fourths of his money and then lost three-fourths of the remainder. He has $6 left. How much money did he start with?

220

Molly and Maggie are Martha's mother's son's wife's daughters. What relation is Martha to Molly and Maggie?

221

In a foreign language, "rota mena lapy" means large apple tree, "rota firg" means small apple, and "mena mola" means large pineapple. Which word means tree?

222

Unscramble the following word:

OMAHGOLR

223

See if you can determine a relationship among the following circles to find the missing number in the last circle.

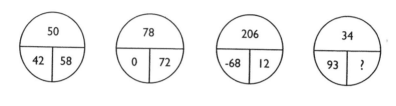

224

What is the missing number in the following series?

(*Hint:* Could the numbers represent something other than quantities?)

13 9 14 4 — 2 5 14 4 9 14 ?

225

Find the hidden phrase or title.

226

What familiar four-letter word can be placed in front of each of the following to form four new words?

Shelf
Worm
Mobile
Mark

227

Given the initial letters of the missing words, complete this sentence:

There are 180 D in a T.

228

In a shuffled deck of 52 playing cards, you alone are picking the cards out of the deck, and the cards are face down. What are the odds of your drawing the Ace, King, Queen, and Jack of spades in succession:

1 chance in 208?
1 chance in 2,704?
1 chance in 6,497,400?
1 chance in 1,000,000,000?

229

What number is 4 times $1/10$ the number that is $1/10$ less than $3/13$?

230

There's an old puzzle that you have probably seen many times where you are asked to assign the same digit for each letter in the following.

$$\begin{array}{r} \text{S E N D} \\ + \text{M O R E} \\ \hline \text{M O N E Y} \end{array}$$

Now try this variation. Let M = 6 and N = 3.

$$\begin{array}{r} \text{S P E N D} \\ - \text{M O R E} \\ \hline \text{M O N E Y} \end{array}$$

231

How many different squares (of any size) are in this figure?

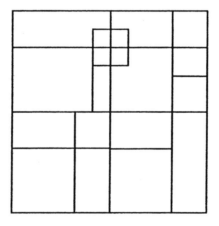

ANSWERS

1. Construct a chart to consider the possible values.

E	1	2	3	4	5	6	7	8	9
Carryovers			1	1	2	2	2	3	3
N	4	8	2	6	0	4	8	2	6
4N + Carryovers	6	2	9	5	2	8	4	1	7

E cannot equal zero since that would make N zero. We need a value where four E's equal N and four N's are equal to E plus a carryover. From the chart, we see that the only place where that occurs is when E equals 2. Therefore, E = 2, N = 8, and O must equal 1, since any number greater than that would result in an additional carryover.

$$
\begin{array}{r}
182 \\
182 \\
182 \\
+182 \\
\hline
728
\end{array}
$$

2. When referring to columns, they are numbered from left to right. In the first column, N + M + S is equal to a number less than 10. Therefore, the greatest number of the three could be a 6 with no carryover from the second column, or a 5 with a carryover from the second column. Obviously, there is a carryover from, or to, at least one of the two middle columns, since their sums yield two different letters.

Let's make an assumption that there is a carryover to the first column, and, therefore, no number can be greater than 5 in that column.

Now consider the possibilities for the last column.

N	1	2	3	4	5
Carryovers				1	
E	3	6	9	2	5

N cannot equal 5, because then E would equal 5. If N = 1, O would have to be 7, which is impossible, since the sum of the second column would then be 23. If N = 3, then O = 1 and U must also be 3, which is impossible. N cannot equal 4 because that would mean that O would equal 1, and both remaining numbers in the first column would be greater than 4. Therefore, N equals 2 and E equals 6.

If N is 2, then O must be 4. Since we accounted for the numbers 2, 3, and 4, M + S can only equal 1 and 5, and they are interchangeable.

```
  2442              2442
  5442              1442
 +1442             +5442
  9326              9326
```

3. Here are three solutions. Can you find others?

```
  8026      8096      8096
    26        96        96
   938       748       758
 +1280     +1980     +1980
 10270     10920     10930
```

4. Since A + B = Z and Z + P = T, it follows that A + B + P = T. We also know that T + A = F, so adding the last two equations and simplifying, we get 2A + B + P = F. We know that B + P + F = 24, so we have:

$$24 - B - P = F$$
$$\underline{2A + B + P = F}$$
$$24 + 2A = 2F \text{ or } 12 + A = F$$

We can replace F with T + A. The equation then becomes 12 + A = T + A, so T = 12 and therefore Q = 19.

5. View C is not correct.

6. Besides the three shown in this puzzle, eight other ways are possible.

7. It is always helpful to set up a legend of what is given and to work from there.

$$X = \$.50 \text{ pens}$$
$$Y = \$5.50 \text{ pens}$$
$$Z = \$9.50 \text{ pens}$$

Set up two equations as follows:

$$X + Y + Z = 100$$
$$\$.50X + \$5.50Y + \$9.50Z = 100$$

Now, we need at least one of the values to drop out in order to consider the other two. Multiply the first equation by – .5 to drop X out of both equations.

$$
\begin{array}{r}
-0.5X \quad -0.5Y \quad -0.5Z = -50 \\
+0.5X \quad +5.5Y \quad +9.5Z = 100 \\
\hline
+5.0Y \quad +9.0Z = \quad 50
\end{array}
$$

$$5Y = 50 - 9Z$$
$$Y = 10 - \frac{9}{5}Z$$

Since we're dealing with whole numbers, Z must be a whole number and a multiple of 5. In this case, Z can only equal 5. With any greater number, Y will become a negative number. So, Z = 5 and Y becomes 1, leaving X to be 94 pens at $.50.

> 94 pens at $.50
> 1 pen at $5.50
> 5 pens at $9.50

8. B, C, and D form the triangle.

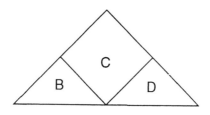

9. Q, K, Q, Q, K, K, and K is the order that works.

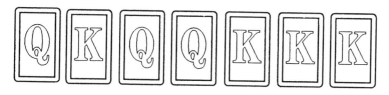

10.

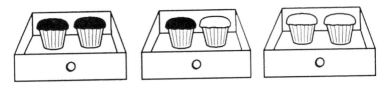

As you can see, there are only three possibilities where a chocolate cupcake could be chosen first.

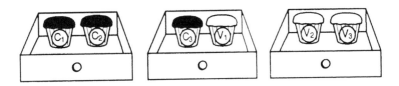

Out of these three, there are only two where a chocolate cupcake could be chosen second.

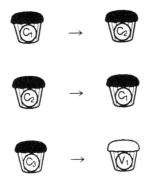

The answer is two out of three.

11. If the first digit of the four-digit code cannot be 0, 5, or 7, that leaves seven possible numbers for the first digit. All ten digits, however, can be used for the second, third, and fourth numbers.

$7 \times 10 \times 10 \times 10$

There are 7,000 possible different codes.

12. Shine

13. The powers of 7 have a repeating pattern for the last digit that can be found easily without performing the entire multiplication of each power.

$$7^0 \quad 7^1 \quad 7^2 \quad 7^3 \quad 7^4 \quad 7^5 \quad 7^6 \quad 7^7$$

$$1 \quad 7 \quad 9 \quad 3 \quad 1 \quad 7 \quad 9 \quad 3$$

With a repeating pattern of four, 7^{32} has the same remainder as 7^0, which is 1. Then 7^{33} would be in the next column, 7^1. Its remainder is 7 when divided by 10.

14. This type of puzzle is a form of syllogism. It can best be shown by using Venn diagrams.

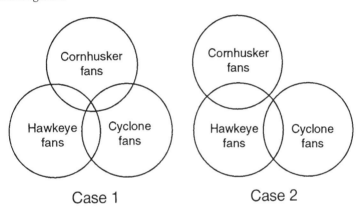

From Case 1, we can see that it is possible for a Cornhusker to be a Cyclone fan, but from Case 2, it is not definite. The conclusion is false.

15. Obviously, their number system is based on something other than 10. Let's say it is based on a notation represented by N.

3N + 0, their number 30, is the number we call 24.

You can reason that 3N + 0 = 24, and N = 8.

Likewise, 3N + 4 = 28, and N = 8.

Their number system is then BASE$_8$ and $5 \times 4 \times 7$, our 140, becomes their 214.

8^2	8^1	8^0
2	1	4

16. Since Dave spoke to the biologist, and Ann was sitting next to the chemist and across from the doctor, Cathy must be the author, and Ann is the biologist. The doctor didn't speak, but Dave did. So, Boobie is the doctor (and was thinking of her own parents) and Dave is the chemist.

17. Turn the first grid 90° to the right, and delete the bottom row of figures. Then turn the result 90° to the right again and delete the bottom row. Do the same with the third grid to get the answer.

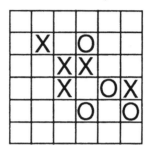

18. The sum is ⅓. Can you determine what the sum is of the infinite series ⅓ + ⅑ + ¹⁄₂₇ + ¹⁄₈₁ . . . ?

19. You can approach this puzzle in several ways.

$$\textbf{REBRAG} = \begin{matrix} \Diamond \\ \Diamond \\ \bigcirc \\ \bigcirc \\ \bigcirc \end{matrix}$$

$$\textbf{LEG} = \Diamond \ \Diamond \ \Diamond$$

One of the first things you may have noticed is that the horizontal figures both contain an L, whereas the two vertical figures contain an R. The equations with two figures both contain a B and the equations with three figures both have a G. The circles have an A and the diamonds an E for their lone vowels. So, that yields this basic information.

L = horizontal	**B = 2**
R = vertical	**A =** ◯
G = 3	**E =** ◇

20. In the first two foreign phrases, roi is the only common word. The word "three" in the English version is likewise the only common word; so, roi means "three." In the second and third foreign phrases, the word kir is used. The English translations share the word meaning "coins." So, kir means coins. Comparing the first and third phrases, we see they share the word kaf, meaning "take." Therefore, kaf means "take." From the English translation of the first phrase, "Kaf navcki roi," we know that navcki means "pieces." From the second phrase, palt must mean "hide," and from the third phrase, inoti means "cautiously."

"Hide pieces cautiously" becomes "Palt navcki inoti," assuming that the foreign syntax follows that of English.

21. The probability is 14.3 percent. Twenty-two percent of the people are not gum chewers and 65 percent are over fifteen years old. Therefore, 22 percent $\times$ 65 percent, or 14.3 percent, are not gum chewers and are above the age of fifteen.

22. The only relationship these capital letters have is that their shapes are totally or partially closed. R is the next and last letter of the alphabet that meets this requirement.

23. The answer is "A is larger than B by 1." This is a good example of reducing a seemingly difficult problem to an example that is workable.

For instance, $2^5 = 32$.

$2^4(16) + 2^3(8) + 2^2(4) + 2^1(2) + 2^0(1) = 31$

That is 1 less than 32.

24. It only took John four steps to accomplish his task.

Step 1—John filled the five-gallon bucket and poured all of it into the six-gallon bucket.

Step 2—He refilled the five-gallon bucket and poured out one gallon into the six-gallon bucket to fill it, leaving four gallons in the five-gallon bucket.

Step 3—He dumped the six-gallon bucket and poured the four gallons from the five-gallon bucket into the six-gallon bucket.

Step 4—Then, John refilled the five-gallon bucket and started home for a piece of cake.

25. The answer is 6119. These four numbers read the same right side up as they do upside down. The numbers on the right are the ones that most closely follow the ones on the left.

26. EMIT spelled backwards is TIME. STAR spelled backwards is RATS.

27. The next number is 4. Here's how to set up the problem.

If the difference of the numbers of the series is taken to the end, a pattern of −3 is established. The next number in the series must yield a −3 in the bottom row. The number next to −8 must be −11. Next to −6 is a −17, and 4 is next to 21.

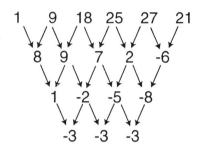

So, here's how we complete the diagram of the setup.

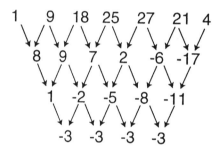

28. In one day, nine men work at a rate of X compared to seven women who work at a rate of Y. This can be expressed as:

$$5(9X + 7Y)$$

Likewise in the second case:

$$4(7X + 11Y)$$

Since these two amounts are equal, we have the following equation:

$$5(9X + 7Y) = 4(7X + 11Y)$$

$$45X + 35Y = 28X + 44Y$$

$$17X = 9Y$$

$$\frac{Y \text{ or women's rate}}{X \text{ or men's rate}} = \frac{17}{9}$$

The women are better workers by a ratio of 17 to 9.

29. The next number is 224. Notice that no digit is greater than 4. That's because these are the $BASE_{10}$ numbers 1, 2, 4, 8, 16, 32, and 64 converted to numbers in $BASE_5$.

30. The missing number is 1. This is the fraction $\frac{1}{7}$ converted to decimal form.

31. The number is 8. Starting with the first and last numbers and working towards the middle, each pair of numbers totals 20.

32. The next number is 30. This is actually two different series contained within one. One series begins with 0 and continues with every other number. Likewise, starting with the 2, a second series is established with every other number.

33. The missing number is 5. Each number stands for a letter of the alphabet where A = 1, B = 2, C = 3, etc. The word spelled out is PUZZLES.

34. The answer is 51. In this problem, the differences between the numbers forms a pattern, allowing you to predict the next numbers. After finding the difference, find the difference of the resulting numbers.

35. The correct number is 51. These numbers represent the answers for each of the six problems starting with Puzzle 29.

36. Unscrambled, the letters spell out ALBERT EINSTEIN.

37. The maximum number of cubes is nineteen.

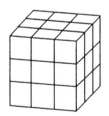

38. There are several different methods of approaching this problem. Since there are three unknowns, it is helpful to establish whatever relationship may exist between the unknowns and then attempt to express that relationship in common terms.

Looking at the first two parts of the equations, we see that § = 2⊗.

We know that ¶ – § = 6 and, therefore, § = ¶ – 6, which means that 2⊗ = ¶ – 6.

If we replace each § with 2⊗, we then have 7⊗ = 2¶.

Solving for ≤ in the third equation, we have $\otimes = \dfrac{\P - 6}{2}$.

Solving for ⊗ in the fourth equation, we have $\otimes = \dfrac{2\P}{7}$.

$$\frac{\P - 6}{2} = \frac{2}{7} \qquad\qquad 3\P = 42$$

$$7(\P - 6) = 4\P \qquad\qquad \P = 14$$

$$7\P - 42 = 4\P \qquad\qquad § = 8$$

$$\otimes = 4$$

39. Each X moves clockwise on the outside squares. Each O moves counterclockwise.

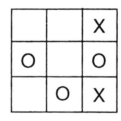

40. From several thousand feet high, the pyramid would look like this. The 60° angle between Lines A and B would appear to be 90° to Judy.

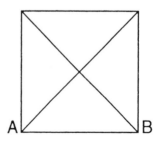

41. Rendrag paid $120 for the entire trip, so for the half of the trip the students were traveling, Rendrag paid $60.00. For the price to be mathematically equitable, the students would each pay $20 to Rendrag for a total of $40. Rendrag's portion for this part of the trip is $20 also.

42. Think of the two figures as an opaque rectangle that has an opaque square behind it. To arrive at the second part of the analogy, the square (the bottom figure) rotates 45° in either direction, and the rectangle (the top figure) rotates 90° in either direction.

To find the correct solution, rotate the rectangle (now the bottom figure) 45°, and rotate the square (now the top figure) 90°. The answer is C.

43. Consider the first figure in the analogy to be two transparent triangles sharing a common base. Let the triangle on the left flip downwards, using the base as an axis. This will give you the second figure. Likewise, in the third figure, let the line connected to the circle on the left fall around the base. C is the answer.

44. A cube is made up of six planes; a tetrahedron has four planes. A triangle has three planes, so it needs two lines to keep it in the same 6 to 4 (3 to 2) ratio. Only A works.

45. In the first two figures of the analogy, place the vertical line of the second figure directly behind the vertical line of the first. Where two flags meet on the same side of the line, they turn into a square on the third figure. Where a flag and a circle meet, they cancel each other out, and no figure appears. If flags or circles are unopposed, they appear as they are on their respective sides of the combined lines. The result is:

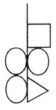

46. C is the only figure that can't be completed with one continuous line that does not retrace any part of the figure.

47. Think it's impossible? It can be done.

The northbound train pulls into the siding, leaving its tail end hanging out on the main track. Meanwhile, the southbound train stays beyond the north switch of the siding, on the main track. When the northbound train stops just short of Point Z (in railroad terms, "in the clear of the main track"), the crew signals the southbound train to proceed south on the main track.

After the southbound train has pulled down fifty or sixty cars, it stops. At Point Z, one of its crew members makes a cut on the fifty or so cars of the southbound train. The southbound train pulls far enough down the main track to allow the northbound train to get out of the siding. The southbound train will have enough room to pull down and not interfere with the cars from the northbound train that are still on the main track.

The crew from the northbound train lines the switch at the top end of the siding, and the northbound train proceeds north, coupling its engine onto the remaining cars of the southbound train. It shoves north, leaving the siding completely. A member of the southbound train's crew lines the bottom end of the siding switch for the main track, and the southbound train pulls its car down two miles or so and stops. Another crew member lines the switch at the top end of the siding for the main track.

The northbound train proceeds south. The engine is pushing its 100 cars and pulling the remaining cars from the southbound train. When the northbound train (now traveling south) gets all its cars past the bottom or southern end of the siding, it lines the siding switch and shoves the remaining cars from the southbound train into the siding. When it comes back out, a crew member lines the switch for the main track, and the train proceeds north with its entire train intact.

The southbound train shoves back to the siding, picks up its remaining cars, and heads south with its entire train. (Hopefully, the crew of the southbound train will line the bottom siding switch for the main track after they pull out, so the next train won't have an open siding switch to worry about.)

48. Border patrol

49. Good with numbers

50. Since Gear R has to make a complete trip around both fixed gears, it doesn't make any difference where we begin. For clarity's sake, we'll start as shown here.

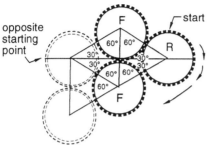

Keep in mind that if Gear R were to revolve around only the top fixed gear, it would make two revolutions, since their diameters are the same. Therefore, Gear R will make one revolution when it reaches the position of the lower left dashed circle.

In order for Gear R to continue to a position opposite its starting point, it needs to travel 60° more, as shown. Since 60°/180° = $\frac{1}{3}$, Gear R makes an additional $\frac{1}{3}$ revolution, for a total of $1\frac{1}{3}$ revolutions to its halfway point. Multiply that by 2 for the whole rotation, and you find that the answer is $2\frac{2}{3}$ revolutions.

51. The question asks for rates. These are usually expressed in units of time, in this case, miles per hour. We are not really interested in the fact that Sara may have traveled two or more hours, because her rate will always be the same.

In one hour, Sara will travel 4 miles down the river. Coming back, against the current, she must travel the same 4 miles, but it will take her two hours to accomplish this. In order to get a rate for one hour, we have to find out how far she traveled against the current in one hour, and that is 2 miles.

Sara travels a total of 6 miles in two hours for a rate of 3 mph. Since she has gone up and down the river, the rate of the river is cancelled out, and Sara's rate is 3 mph (6 miles divided by two hours) in still water, which means the rate of the river is 1 mph.

52. Candace is Jane's niece.

53. In a twelve-hour period starting after either 6 a.m. or 6 p.m., there will be eleven times when the hands are directly opposite each other. Twelve hours divided by eleven equals 1 hour, 5 minutes, and $27\frac{3}{11}$ seconds. Go back the 1 hour, 5 minutes, and $27\frac{3}{11}$ seconds from 6 o'clock, and you get 4:54 and $32\frac{8}{11}$ seconds.

54. The missing letter is R. The letters spell out "What is the answer?"

55. The sum of the three numbers below the diameter equals $\frac{1}{3}$ of the top number. So, the answer is one.

56. Ten weights will balance either 50 gold coins or 40 silver coins. Since only 20 gold coins are used, that means the weight of 30 gold coins is to be used by the silver coins. The weights are in a 4-to-5 ratio, and $\frac{4}{5}$ of 30 = 24. So, 24 silver coins should be added to the 20 gold coins to balance the 10 weights.

57. Here are the answers.

A = 3
B = 1
C = 4
D = 2

58. The 2-inch hose will drain the water faster, since it has a bigger spout area than the two 1-inch hoses. The area of a circle is given by multiplying π (3.14) times the radius squared. The radius of the 2-inch hose is 1 inch. Its area is equal to $\pi \times 1 \times 1$ or π square inches. The area of the two 1-inch hoses is:

$$\pi \times \tfrac{1}{2} \times \tfrac{1}{2} \ + \pi \times \tfrac{1}{2} \times \tfrac{1}{2}$$

or $\pi/4 + \pi/4$, which equals $\pi/2$ square inches

The 2-inch hose drains water twice as fast.

59.

$$
\begin{array}{r}
41067 \\
\underline{41607} \\
\$826743
\end{array}
$$

60.

$$
\begin{array}{rr}
6 & 2174 \\
\underline{+\ 6} & \underline{2980} \\
12 & 5154
\end{array}
$$

61. The numbers are the numbers on the telephone, as shown here.

ABC	DEF	GHI	JKL	MNO	PRS	TUV	WXY
2	3	4	5	6	7	8	9

If the number is slanted to the left, then the left-most letter of that grouping is the letter to be used. If it is slanted to the right, the right-most letter is the choice. Letters that are straight up and down are represented by the center letter.

The note says, "Went to buy a new phone."

62. If 81 students had taken a course in geography, then only 9 students out of the 90 (10 took neither) took only geology. Since 63 students out of 90 had taken geology, that leaves 27 who had taken only geography.

27 + 9 = 36 $^{36}/_{100}$ is 36 percent

The answer is 36 percent or nine out of twenty-five.

Since 36 students took either geography or geology and 10 took neither, that leaves 54 percent who took at least one class in both.

63. Unfinished Symphony

64. Although the chances are remote, you just might pull the 24 blue socks out first. You'd need two more to make certain to get two black socks. You'd be assured of a pair of black socks by pulling 26 socks.

65. The first two digits enclosed within any parentheses are added together to get the second number contained within each parentheses. To get the first two digits of any following parentheses, add the numbers found in the preceding parentheses together. In this case, that is:

37:10

66. Dashing through the snow

67. Let's take a look at how this might be accomplished. Each letter represents a different person present at the gathering. Remember that when one person shakes another's hand, each person gets credit for a handshake. There are several ways to accomplish this. Here's one.

X shakes hands with W, Y, Z, T.
Y shakes hands with W, Z, T, X.
W shakes hands with Z, T, X, Y.
Z shakes hands with R, X, Y, W.
T shakes hands with S, X, Y, W.

As can be seen from our chart, X, Y, W, Z, and T each have four handshakes. R and S each have one. So the minimum number of people needed to accomplish the required handshakes is seven. X, Y, W, Z, and T each have four handshakes, and R and S have one apiece for a total of twenty-two handshakes.

68. Below is a table showing different combinations and probabilities of the dice. From the total combinations, we can see that there are a total of thirty-six chances.

Total Number Showing on Dice	Total Combinations	Chances
2	1	1/36
3	2	2/36
4	3	3/36
5	4	4/36
6	5	5/36
7	6	6/36
8	5	5/36
9	4	4/36
10	3	3/36
11	2	2/36
12	1	1/36

You can see there are three ways to roll a 10 and six ways to roll a 7. Out of these nine possibilities, three are favorable for a win. Therefore, the chances for winning with 10 as a point are one in three.

69. Let's work this out.

Obviously, 10 must be in the top row, but it cannot be in either of the first two positions, since that would result in a duplication of 5's. Since 7 can only result from either 8 – 1 or 9 – 2, 8 and 9 must be in the top or next row. Nine can only result from 10 – 1, or it has to be in the top row. Therefore, 8 and 9 are not in the same row, and neither are 1 and 2, but all four numbers are in the top two rows. Out of the seven positions in the top two rows, we have 10, 9, 8, 1, 2, and 5 with 7 in the third row. That leaves 6, 3, or 4 for the remaining position in the top row. The digit next to the 7 can't be a 6 because that would result in duplicate 1's, and 6 cannot be the result of 7 minus any other number. Therefore, 6 is the remaining number of the seven numbers in the top two rows.

Six cannot be next to 5 or above 7, so it must be in the top row with 10. But 6 cannot be next to 10, so it is in the first or second position of the top row. And the number next to it must be 1. That means 9 cannot be in the top row; it would have to be next to 10, which would result in double 1's when subtracted. Eight must then be the other number in the top row.

That means the top row is 6 1 10 8, from which the remaining numbers can be generated:

6 1 10 8
5 9 2
4 7
3

For numbers 1 through 15:

13 3 15 14 6
10 12 1 8
2 11 7
9 4
5

70. The two winning first moves are these.

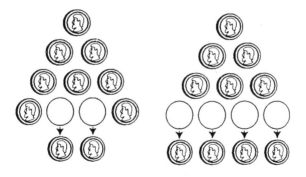

71. Here's one way the letter cross could look.

$$4265$$
$$8$$
$$3$$
$$1790$$

The total of the numbers used is 51 (17 × 3). The total of the numbers 1 through 9 is 45. There is a difference of 6. That difference is found in the letters D and G, since they are the only two letters counted twice. D and G must equal 6, and E + F must equal 11 to total 17 in the column. Since A = 4, D and G must be 1 and 5. The number 7 cannot be E or F. It would require the 4 to total 11. Also, 7 cannot be B, C, or D, since 4 + 7 would require the remaining two numbers in the top row to total 6, which is impossible. Therefore, 7 is in the bottom row with 0. That means the bottom row needs two numbers (besides 7 and 0) to total 10 for G + H + I + J to equal 17. One of those numbers must be 1 or 5. It can't be 5. You'd then have two 5's to total 10. Therefore, D = 5, G = 1, and the remaining number in the bottom row is 9. At this point the puzzle looks like this.

$$4BC5$$
$$E$$
$$F$$
$$1790$$

E + F must equal 11. The possible combinations are as follows.

$$2 + 9$$
$$3 + 8$$
$$4 + 7$$
$$5 + 6$$

The only possibility out of this group is 3 + 8, solving the values for D, E, F, and G, leaving 6 and 2 for B and C.

72. The next one is 46656.

Disregarding the number 1, these are the four consecutive lowest numbers that are both cubes and squares.

64	729	4,096
8^2 or 4^3	27^2 or 9^3	64^2 or 16^3
15,625	and the fifth,	**46,656**
125^2 or 25^3		216^2 or 36^3

73. Here's how to find the answer.

Since we know that Box C isn't the smallest, out of Boxes A, B, C, and D, Box D is the smallest. Its number is either 4 or 5.

The possible numbers for Box C are 2, 3, or 4 (not the largest or the smallest).

Box A can only be 2 or 3, since it is bigger than Box C or Box D, but it is not the biggest.

The total of Box C plus Box D must be at least 6 but not more than 7. The greatest possible sum of two different numbers between 1 and 5 is 7, assuming that sum is the equal to the sum of two other different numbers.

Since Box A is 2 or 3, and its number plus Box E's number must be at least 6, Box E is either 4 or 5.

Box A = 2 or 3
Box C = 2 or 3
Box D = 4 or 5
Box E = 4 or 5

We know that Box A is bigger than Box C, so Box A = 2, Box C = 3, Box D = 4, Box E = 5, and Box B = 1.

74. Three out of eight chances. Here are the possibilities.

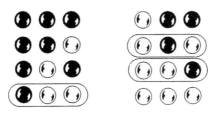

So, there are only three chances out of the eight possible combinations you could make.

75. Believe it or not, fifteen pieces (maximum) will result with four straight cuts through a cube.

This formula will give you the answer for any number of cuts. N = the number of cuts. So, three planar cuts yield eight pieces, four planar cuts yield fifteen pieces, five planar cuts yield twenty-six pieces, and six planar cuts yield forty-two pieces, and so on.

$$\left(\frac{N^3 + 5N}{6}\right) +1 = \text{Number of Pieces}$$

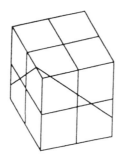

76. Let's see how it's done. You only need to move five coins to turn the triangle upside down.

    1—Move 3 to Row 3, outside 4.

    2—Move 2 to Row 3, outside 6.

    3—Move 1 to Row 6, between 12 and 13.

    4—Move 15 to Row 6, between 13 and 14.

    5—Move 11 to be the lone coin on the point of the upside-down triangle.

In general, where N is equal to the length of any side of a triangle (length in number of coins), the minimum number of coins that need to be moved to turn that triangle upside down can be found by this formula.

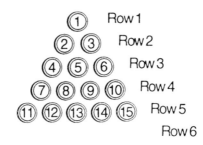

$$\frac{N\,(N+1)}{6}$$

If the result of the division has a remainder, the answer is simply rounded down to the nearest whole number found in the quotient.

For example, if N = 7, then $\frac{7 \times 8}{6}$ = 6 $\overline{)56}$ = 9.

Rounding down to 9 will give the minimum number of coins needed to be moved in a triangle that has seven coins on a side.

Special thanks to mathematician Frank Bernhart (Rochester, N.Y.) for his assistance.

77. Here are the remaining moves.

      7—Move 1 to 4.

      8—Move 15 to 6.

      9—Move 6 to 13.

    10—Move 12 to 14.

    11—Move 4 to 13.

    12—Move 14 to 12.

    13—Move 11 to 13.

78. Regardless of which face of Cube 1 you start with, the tunnel cannot exit through Cubes 3, 5, or 8.

79. This object requires six cubes to build. Here is its orthographic projection and the sixth side.

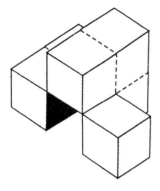
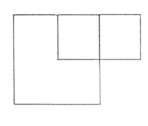

80. A man among men

81. Here's one way.

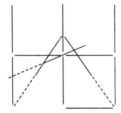

82. Far be it from me

83. If you are not careful, this short logic puzzle can be very confusing. Often, a solver's first instinct is to compare the speed and strength of each of the friends to determine their nicknames. Further inspection reveals that there isn't enough information to solve the puzzle that way. Here's where a grid of possibilities comes in handy.

We'll use X's and O's to fill in the grids. O will represent an elimination, and X will be a definite selection.

From a, we know that Pat can't be either Rabbit or Fly. So he must be either Bear or Walleye. We know from b that Tom cannot be either Rabbit or Walleye. So he must be either Bear or Fly. So, let's begin to fill in the chart.

	Rabbit	Fly	Walleye	Bear
Bob				
Bill				
Pat	O	O		
Tom	O		O	

From c, we know that Bob can't be Bear or Rabbit. Since he is faster than both Pat and Bear, Pat must be Walleye (since Pat was either Walleye or Bear).

As you can see from the final chart, Bill must be Rabbit, Tom has to be Bear, and Bob must be Fly.

	Rabbit	Fly	Walleye	Bear
Bob	O	X	O	O
Bill	X	O	O	O
Pat	O	O	X	O
Tom	O	O	O	X

84. We know that Brand A and Brand B equal 40 pounds. We also know that 40 pounds times $7 a pound will equal $280. We can set up two equations that can be solved simultaneously.

$$A + B = 40 \text{ pounds}$$
$$9A + 4B = \$280$$

Multiply the first equation by −9 to cancel out the A's.

$$-9A - 9B = -360$$
$$\underline{9A + 4B = 280}$$
$$-5B = -80$$

B = 16 and, therefore, A = 24 pounds.

85. Here's how you figure it out.

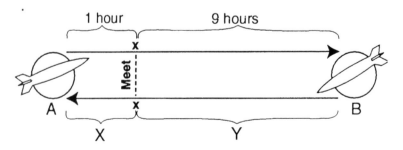

$X + Y$ = total distance
V_f = velocity of faster rocket
V_s = velocity of slower rocket
T_b = time before meeting
Y = velocity of the faster rocket multiplied by the time before they meet $(V_f \times T_b)$
X = velocity of the slower rocket multiplied by the time before they meet $(V_s \times T_b)$

$$\text{Therefore,} \quad \frac{X}{Y} = \frac{V_s}{V_f}$$

Now after the rockets meet, Y is equal to the slower velocity multiplied by 9, and X is equal to the faster velocity multiplied by one.

$$\text{Thus:} \quad \frac{X}{Y} = \frac{V_f}{9V_s}$$

We now have two different fractions that represent $\frac{X}{Y}$, and they are equal.

$$\frac{V_s}{V_f} = \frac{V_f}{9V_s}$$
$$V_f^2 = 9V_s^2$$
$$\sqrt{V_f^2} = \sqrt{9V_s^2}$$
$$V_f = 3V_s$$

The faster rocket is going three times as fast as the slower rocket.

86. Let's call the first system X and the second system Y.

X	Y
14	36
133	87

In order to get an idea of some relationship between the two systems, we'll subtract 14 from 133 (119) and compare that to the difference of 87 minus 36 (51). We can compare 119 to 51, but first, let's reduce it by dividing by 17, giving us 7 to 3. For every seven degrees on the X thermometer, Y will grow or decrease by three. When X is at 14°, if we move toward X becoming 0°, Y will be reduced by 6°. When X is 0°, Y = 30°, giving us the formula Y = $\frac{3}{7}$X + 30.

To find the temperature at which both thermometers read the same, set Y to equal X, and the formula then becomes:

$$X = \tfrac{3}{7}X + 30$$
$$\tfrac{4}{7}X = 30$$
$$4X = 210$$
$$X = 52.5°$$

87. There are three different shapes to consider: a square, a loop, and two connecting lines. Figures A, B, and C each use two of the shapes. These first three figures form a pattern. Beginning with Figure D, the sequence continues. To get Figure D, Figure A was rotated 90° to the right. Figure E is really Figure B rotated 90° to the right. Therefore, the sixth figure will be Figure C rotated 90° to the right.

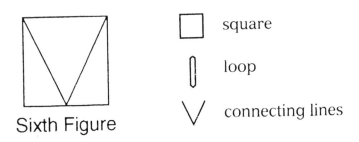

Sixth Figure

□ square

▯ loop

∨ connecting lines

88. The answer is D. The other four figures have both concave and convex components. Figure D has convex parts only.

89. The only thing you have to go on are the names of the people and the letters in their names. After a little inspection, you'll find each letter of the name is equivalent to three of "them," whatever "them" may be. Mary Les has seven letters in her name, therefore she has twenty-one of "them."

90. There are twenty-five individual cubes.

91. This is a good example of a problem or puzzle that can be broken into smaller components to determine a pattern.

If one person walks into a theater to take one seat, that person has only one choice. If two people occupy two seats, this can happen in two different ways. Three people occupying three seats (following the condition that each subsequent person sits next to another) can be accomplished in four different ways. Four people in four seats produce eight ways. We'll make a table to see what we have.

Number of People	Possible Combinations
1	1
2	2
3	4
4	8
5	?

As can be seen, with each additional person and seat, the different orders increase by a power of two. For five people in five seats, there are sixteen different possible combinations. For any number N, it can be seen that $2^{(N-1)}$ will give the correct answer. So, for twelve people, 4096 different combinations are possible:

$$2^{(13-1)} = 2^{12} = 4096$$

92. There were 20 nickels and 20 dimes. To solve this, set up the following equations, where n = nickels and d = dimes:

$$n = d$$
$$.05n + .10d = 3.00$$
$$.05n + .10n = 3.00$$
$$.15n = 3.00$$
$$n = 20$$

93. $x = 5$, $y = 6$, and $z = 4$, so the sum is 15. The variable x can be either 0 or 5. It must be 5 because there is no number that ends in 0 when multiplied by 7 ($y \times 7$, resulting in x). Therefore, a 3 is carried over to the y. Since x is 5, y must be 6 because $7 \times 6 = 42$. Add the 3 that was carried over and you get 45. Therefore, z is 4.

94. It might be helpful to set up a grid as follows:

	Basketball	Football	Baseball
Alex	x		o
Ryan	o		
Steven	x	o	x

We can see that Ryan must like basketball since neither Alex nor Steven does. Steven does not like basketball or baseball, so he must like football, leaving Alex liking baseball.

95. Seven zips have the weight of 1 wob. The problem can be set up as follows:

$$26z = 4c + 2w$$
$$8z + 2c = 2w$$

Rearranging, we get

$$(1)\ 26z = 4c + 2w$$
$$(2)\ 8z = -2c + 2w$$

Multiply equation (2) by 2 so that the c factor drops out, and combine the two equations:

$$
\begin{aligned}
26z &= 4c + 2w \\
\underline{16z} &= \underline{-4c + 4w} \\
42z &= 6w \\
7z &= w
\end{aligned}
$$

96. Look before you leap

97. The missing number is 10. The numbers in each circle add up to 50.

98. The answer is 96. Set up the following equations:

$$\tfrac{1}{2} \times \tfrac{2}{3} \times \tfrac{3}{5} = \tfrac{6}{30} = \tfrac{1}{5}$$
$$\tfrac{1}{5} \times 240 = 48$$
$$48 \div \tfrac{1}{2} = 96$$

99. It's the right thing to do.

100. The answer is "three words."

101. The next letter is P. The letters missing between letters in the series form the pattern 1, 2, 1, 2, 1, 2…

102. Figure 4 is the only one that doesn't contain a triangle.

103. The lesser of two evils

104. It is impossible to average 60 miles per hour for this trip. At 30 miles per hour, the car would travel one mile in two minutes; at 60 miles per hour, the car would travel two miles in two minutes. So, in order to average 60 mph, the entire trip of two miles would have to be completed in two minutes. But the driver has already used two minutes going from point A to point B; there's not time left to get from point B to point C.

105. Here's one way to solve the puzzle:

TOOK
BOOK
BOON
BORN
BURN

106. 6.25 percent. Remember, length × width = area. Let l = length and w = width. Then

$$l + .25l = 1.25l$$
$$w - .25w = .75w$$
$$1.25l \times .75w = 93.75lw$$

Finally,

$$100 - 93.75 = 6.25$$

107. The chances are 1 in 3. Here are all the possible draws (C1 = first cherry gumdrop, C2 = second cherry gumdrop, O = orange gumdrop):

First draw	Second draw
C1	C2
C1	O
C2	C1
C2	O
O	C1
O	C2

Among the six possible draws, O appears twice in the second draw column; thus the chances are 2 in 6, or 1 in 3.

108. Five.

109. The "R" goes above the line. The letters above the line are closed with a space inside them.

110. Time slips into the future

111. There are 100 years in a century.

112. Let x = the fraction. Then:
$$(3 \times (\tfrac{1}{4})x) \times x = \tfrac{1}{12}$$
$$(3/4)x^2 = \tfrac{1}{12}$$
$$x^2 = \tfrac{1}{9}$$
$$x = \tfrac{1}{3}$$

113. Two miles. They are actually eating up the distance at 120 miles per hour (50 + 70):
$$\frac{120 \text{ miles}}{60 \text{ minutes}} = \text{two miles in one minute}$$

114. Pocket full of money

115. They can be combined in 12 different ways.

116. $\tfrac{1}{24}$
$$\frac{3}{32} - \frac{1}{16} = \frac{1}{32}$$
$$4 \times \left(\frac{1}{3} \times \frac{1}{32} \right) = \frac{4}{96} \text{ or } \frac{1}{24}$$

117. The letters "mot" will create the words "mother," "motion," "motor," "motif," and "motto."

118. The answer is (e). Remember, x may be a negative number.

119. He would have 20 pleezorns. Count the letters in each name and multiply by 2.

120. .1 × .9 × .8 = .072 = 7.2%

121. Line dance

122. The ratio is 1 to 2. One way to solve this problem is to set up an equation in which x equals the amount of $48 chemical used and y equals the amount of $36 chemical used:

$$48x + 36y = 40(x + y)$$
$$48x + 36y = 40x + 40y$$
$$8x = 4y$$
$$\frac{x}{y} = \frac{1}{2}$$

123. Traffic jam

124. There are 31 triangles.

125. The ratio is 1 to 2. It might help to set up the problem as follows:

$$\frac{5x}{4y} = \frac{7}{8}$$
$$40x = 28y$$
$$10x = 7y$$

Thus, $10x$ to $7y$ is a 1-to-1 relationship. We are asked for the ratio of $10x$ to $14y$; since $14 = 7 \times 2$, we can see that it is a 1-to-2 relationship.

126. Don't count your chickens before they hatch.

127. Three-ring circus

128. Here are 21 four-letter words:

twin	wine	lint
kiln	kilt	lent
wink	wilt	like
link	welt	kine
tine	tile	lien
newt	kite	line
went	wile	knit

129. The answer is 13,222.

$$12,000$$
$$+1,222$$
$$13,222$$

130. JJ. The letters are the initial letters of pairs of month names, starting with October-November.

131. Forward thinking

132. Double-decker sandwich

133. Draw a line as follows and you'll see the answer, June:

JOKE / JUNE

134. $4^6 + 6^4$ . . . by more than double

135. Microorganism

136. There is one wheel on a unicycle.

137. Fifteen angles of less than 90 degrees can be formed.

138. Here they are:

$$\frac{1}{2} = \frac{6{,}729}{13{,}458}$$

$$\frac{1}{3} = \frac{5{,}832}{17{,}496}$$

$$\frac{1}{4} = \frac{4{,}392}{17{,}568}$$

$$\frac{1}{5} = \frac{2{,}769}{13{,}845}$$

$$\frac{1}{6} = \frac{2{,}943}{17{,}658}$$

$$\frac{1}{7} = \frac{2{,}394}{16{,}758}$$

$$\frac{1}{8} = \frac{3{,}187}{25{,}496}$$

$$\frac{1}{9} = \frac{6{,}381}{57{,}429}$$

139. i before e except after c

140. The missing numbers are 18 and 5, respectively. There are actually two separate series of numbers in this puzzle. Look at every other number, beginning first with 8 and then with 15.

141. The value of z must be 9 in all cases.

142. The value of x is 1. The variable y can have any of a number of values, but x must always equal 1 and z must always equal 9.

143. Yes. A number is divisible by 8 if its last three digits are divisible by 8. Examples: 6,240; 9,184; 15,536.

144. Doorbell. All the rest have handles.

145. You would write it 17 times. Don't forget that there are two 4s in 44!

146. Figure C is the only figure without a straight line.

147. Right cross followed by an uppercut

148. For these three numbers, 455 is the lowest common denominator.

149. Fill in the blanks

150. 107 percent of 300 is greater. Because 107 percent is equivalent to 1.07, we have

$$1.07 \times 300 = 321$$
$$.50 \times 600 = 300$$

151. The answer is $^{10}/_{33}$. The problem can be solved as follows:

$$\cfrac{1}{3+\cfrac{1}{3\frac{1}{3}}} = \cfrac{1}{3+\cfrac{1}{\frac{10}{3}}} = \cfrac{1}{3+\cfrac{3}{10}} = \cfrac{1}{\frac{33}{10}} = \frac{10}{33}$$

152.

1	8	13	12
14	11	2	7
4	5	16	9
15	10	3	6

153. Here's one way:

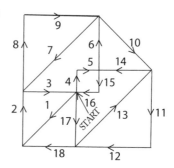

154. You would receive 221 silver pieces. If you were to exchange your kooklas only for gold, it would require 40×7 or 280 pieces. But there are only 161 gold pieces, leaving you 119 gold pieces short. The value of silver coins to gold coins is in the ratio of 13 to 7:

$$\frac{13}{7} = \frac{x}{119}$$

$$7x = 1{,}547$$

$$x = 221$$

155. The missing number is 35. The second number in each box is the square of the first number minus 1.

156. There are 720 possible arrangements. Use the following equation to solve the problem (this is called factorial notation):

$$6! = 6 \times 5 \times 4 \times 3 \times 2 \times 1 = 720$$

157. Hole in one

158. The number 9 goes below the line and the number 10 goes above it—the numbers 1, 2, 6, and 10 are all spelled with three letters; the rest have four or more.

159. Your eyes are bigger than your stomach

160. Here are two examples:
  1. When giving yes and no answers, a person who tells a lie about a lie is telling the truth.
  2. Imagine a child rolling his wagon backward down a hill. If you were to film this and run the film backward, you would see the wagon going forward up the hill.

161. Algebra

162. $8\frac{88}{88}$

163. There are 24 cubes.

164. They say at least 100 words can be made from "Thanksgiving." How many can you find?

165. It is $7/9$. The problem can be approached as follows:

$$1/10 \div 1/2 \div 1/5 = 1/10 \times 2 \times 5 = 1$$
$$1 \times 7/9 = 7/9$$

166. Elbow grease

167. x, y, and z = 8, 12, and 60 pounds, respectively. Starting with the 8 ft. section:

$$8 \text{ ft.} \times 10 \text{ lbs.} = 80 \text{ ft.-lbs.}$$

To balance, the bottom left part of the mobile must also equal 80 ft.-lbs., so its total weight must be 20 lbs. (4 ft. × 20 lbs. = 80 ft.-lbs.) Therefore,

$$x + y = 20$$
and
$$6x = 4y.$$
So, $y = 20 - x$
and substituting,
$$6x = 4(20 - x)$$
$$6x = 80 - 4x$$
$$10x = 80$$
$$x = 8$$
and therefore,
$$y = 12.$$

Adding the total weights of the left side, we have
$$120 + 10 + 8 + 12 = 150 \text{ lbs.}$$
$$150 \text{ lbs.} \times 4 \text{ ft.} = 600 \text{ ft.-lbs.}$$
Therefore, the right side must also be 600 ft.-lbs.:
$$10 \text{ ft.} \times z \text{ lbs.} = 600 \text{ ft.-lbs.}$$
$$z = 60$$

168. All answers are divisible by nine.

169. The square is 6 feet by 6 feet. To solve this problem, let x represent each side of the square. Then

$$4x = x^2 \times \frac{2}{3}$$
$$12x = 2x^2$$
$$6x = x^2$$
$$x = 6$$

170. Shrinking violets

171. 2 in 9. Because each die has 6 faces, there are 6 × 6 or 36 possible combinations of numbers. Of these, 6 combinations result in a 7:

6 and 1
1 and 6
5 and 2
2 and 5
4 and 3
3 and 4

And 2 combinations result in an 11:

5 and 6
6 and 5

thus the chances are 8 in 36, or 2 in 9.

172. Calm before the storm

173.

MOOD
MOON
MORN
BORN
BARN

174. T = 15. Since A = 2, we can substitute A into the first four equations to come up with the following:

(1)	2 + B	= H
(2)	H + P	= T
(3)	T + 2	= F
(4)	B + P + F	= 30

Now substitute equation (1) into equation (2):

$$(2 + B) + P = T$$

Rearranging, we get

$$B + P = T - 2$$

Substitute this into equation (4):

$$(T - 2) + F = 30$$

Finally, substitute equation (3) into equation (4) and solve for T:

$$(T - 2) + (T + 2) = 30$$
$$2T = 30$$
$$T = 15$$

175. An onion costs 7 cents. Set up the equations, with x as potatoes and y as onions:

$$5x + 6y = 1.22$$
$$6x + 5y = 1.31$$

Multiply the first equation by 6, the second one by 5:

$$30x + 36y = 7.32$$
$$30x + 25y = 6.55$$

Subtract the second equation from the first, and you have:

$$0x + 11y = .77$$
$$y = .07$$

176. Rising tide

177. It can be done as follows:

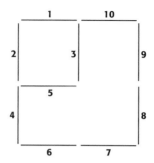

178. A: $\dfrac{343}{1000}$ B: $\dfrac{7}{24}$

On any given single draw with all 10 balls in the box, there is a 7 in 10 chance of drawing a green ball. So the probability of all 3 balls chosen being green is:

$$\frac{7}{10} \times \frac{7}{10} \times \frac{7}{10} = \frac{343}{1000} = 34.3\%$$

If the balls are not replaced in the bag:

The chance on the first draw is 7 in 10; on the second draw, it is 6 in 9; and on the third draw, it is 5 in 8. So the probability of 3 balls being pulled in succession if they are not replaced is:

$$\frac{7}{10} \times \frac{6}{9} \times \frac{5}{8} = \frac{210}{720} \text{ or } \frac{7}{24} = 29.2\%$$

179. The missing number is zero. If you convert each fraction to twelfths, you get the following series:

$$\frac{5}{12} \quad \frac{4}{12} \quad \frac{3}{12} \quad \frac{2}{12} \quad \frac{1}{12} \quad 0$$

180. Multiplication tables

181. There are 206 bones in the human body.

182. Factors of the number 12 (6 + 4 + 3 + 2 + 1) add up to 16.

183. 18. ¼ of ⅓ of ⅙ is ¹⁄₇₂; ¹⁄₇₂ of 432 is 6; and 6 divided by ⅓ is 18.

184. Deep in thought

185. Fifty-six applicants have experience in selling both golf equipment and athletic shoes. Since 13 of the applicants have had no sales experience, we're dealing with 87 people who have some experience. Of the 87 applicants, 65 of them have sold golf equipment, which means that 22 of this group haven't sold golf equipment (87 − 65 = 22). Seventy-eight of the applicants have sold shoes, which means that 9 haven't (87 − 78 = 9). Therefore, we have 9 + 22 or 31 people who could not have sold both—thus, 87 − 31 = 56 people who *have* had experience in selling both.

186. 110 square yards. An area 11 yards square measures 11 yards on each of four sides and therefore has a total of 121 square yards. An area of 11 square yards, if it were square, would be just under 3.32 yards on each side. The difference between the two, then, is found by subtracting 11 square yards from 121 square yards: 110 square yards.

187. Life

188. You are on time

189. 6009, 6119

190. Seven. These are the elements hydrogen, carbon, and nitrogen, with their respective atomic numbers; seven is the atomic number for nitrogen.

191. Can't see the forest for the trees

192. They are 496 and 8,128. The next perfect number after that is 33,550,336!

193. There are 16 possibilities, each having a probability of ¹/₁₆. There are 6 ways with exactly 2 tails, 4 ways with 3 tails, and 1 way with 4 tails. That's a total of 11 ways out of 16. The chances are 11 in 16.

HHHH	TTTT
HTTT	THHH
HHHT	TTTH
HTHH	THTT
HHTH	THHT
HHTT	TTHH
HTHT	THTH
HTTH	THHT

194. A break in the action

195. Let a smile be your umbrella.

196. 27,000. The repeating pattern is, respectively, 2, 3, and 5 times the preceding number.

197.

198. It will take 1.2 hours.

The equation can be set up this way:

$$\frac{x}{3} + \frac{x}{2} = 1$$

Multiply by 6:

$$2x + 3x = 6$$
$$5x = 6$$
$$x = \frac{6}{5} = 1.2$$

199. I am 19 years old and my sister is 9.

Let x = my sister's age and y = my age.

$$y = x + 10 \text{ and}$$
$$y + 1 = 2(x + 1)$$
$$y = 2x + 1$$

Substituting this result in our first equation, we have

$$2x + 1 = x + 10$$
$$x = 9$$
$$\text{so}$$
$$y = 19.$$

When my sister was 5, I was 3 times older than she was.

200. The missing letter is S. These are the first letters of the even numbers when spelled out, beginning with two.

201. Upside-down cake

202. Sally Billingsley and Susie Jenkins are the real names. Because one of the first two statements had to be false, the third statement also had to be false.

203. The square of 95 is 9,025. There are several ways this can be done. Here's one way. It helps to remember that any number ending in 5, when squared, will always end in 25.

Go to the number ending in 0 directly above the number ending in 5—in this case 100. Now go to the number ending in 0 directly below the number ending in 5—in this case 90.

In your mind square 100 (10,000) and square 90 (8,100). Add these two numbers together (18,100) and divide by 2 (9,050); then replace the last two digits with 25. So the square of 95 is 9,025.

Now, come up with another way to do this.

204. The missing letter is N; the word is "sandwich."

205. Power surge

206. None. Instead, turn the puzzle upside-down and add:

$$
\begin{array}{r}
86 \\
91 \\
+68 \\
\hline
245
\end{array}
$$

207. 20 percent. Say there are 10 caramels. Since the number of caramels is 25 percent of the number of other candies, there must be 40 pieces of candy that aren't caramels. The total number of pieces of candy = 10 + 40 = 50, so $^{10}/_{50}$ = $^{1}/_{5}$ = 20 percent.

208. Fender bender

209. There are 118 elements in the periodic table.

210. Here's one way to solve the puzzle:

ROAD
ROAM
ROOM
LOOM
LOOP

211. Diagram E is the odd one out. The other four are symmetrical about both of their axes; if you turn them 90 degrees, they will look the same as in their original positions.

212.

C	=	100
D	=	500
M	=	1,000
$\overline{V}$	=	5,000
$\overline{X}$	=	10,000
$\overline{L}$	=	50,000
$\overline{C}$	=	100,000
$\overline{D}$	=	500,000
$\overline{M}$	=	1,000,000

213. Current affair

214. Here are some 10-letter words.

Typewriter	Proprietor	Tetterwort
Pepperroot	Pirouetter	Repertoire
Pepperwort	Prerequire	Perpetuity

215. Central Intelligence Agency

216. The chances are still 1 in 50.

217. The missing number is $1/30$. The series is constructed as follows:

$$12 = 1/7 \text{ of } 84$$
$$2 = 1/6 \text{ of } 12$$
$$2/5 = 1/5 \text{ of } 2$$
$$1/10 = 1/4 \text{ of } 2/5$$
$$1/30 = 1/3 \text{ of } 1/10$$

218. Guilty beyond a reasonable doubt

219. $96. Use the equation

$$(1/4)x - (3/4 \times (1/4)x) = \$6$$
$$(1/4)x - (3/16)x = \$6$$

Multiply each side by 16:

$$4x - 3x = \$96$$
$$x = \$96$$

220. She is their aunt.

221. "Lapy" means tree. From the first two phrases, "rota" must mean apple. From the third phrase, "mena" must mean large, leaving "lapy" to be tree.

222. Hologram

223. The numbers in each circle add up to 150, so the missing number is 23.

224. The missing number is 7. The numbers have a one-to-one correspondence with the letters of the alphabet, where A = 1, B = 2, C = 3, and so forth. The word spelled out is "mind-bending."

225. No time left on the clock

226. Book

227. There are 180 degrees in a triangle.

228. The chance of drawing the ace of spades is 1 in 52; for the king, 1 in 51; for the queen, 1 in 50; and for the jack, 1 in 49. To calculate the answer, multiply these all together:

$1/52 \times 1/51 \times 1/50 \times 1/49 = 1/6{,}497{,}400$

229.

$34/650$ or $17/325$

$1/10$ less than $3/13$ is:

$30/130 - 13/130 = 17/130$

4 times $1/10$ of that number is:

$4 \times 1/10 \times 17/130 = 4/10 \times 17/130$

$= 2/50 \times 17/130$

$= 34/650$

$= 17/325$

230.

$$\begin{array}{r} 70{,}839 \\ -\ 6{,}458 \\ \hline 64{,}381 \end{array}$$

The answer to the "SEND + MORE = MONEY" puzzle is:

$$\begin{array}{r} 9{,}567 \\ +\ 1{,}085 \\ \hline 10{,}652 \end{array}$$

231. There are 19 squares.